THE PRAYER OF LOVE
AND SILENCE

Our cloisters are schools of
charity, of silence and of liberty

Dom Innocent Le Masson,
50th General of the Carthusian Order
(1675–1703)

THE PRAYER OF LOVE
AND SILENCE

by a Carthusian

Translated from the French
by a
Monk of Parkminster

GRACEWING

First published in 1962 by Darton, Longman and Todd Ltd,
this edition published 2006

Gracewing Publishing
2 Southern Avenue, Leominster
Herefordshire HR6 0QF

ISBN 0 85244 673 X
ISBN 978 0 85244 673 7

Imprimi potest: Fr Ferdinandus, Prior Cartusiae:
in domo Cartusiae in festo S. Joannis Baptistae 1960.
Nihil obstat: Joannes M. T. Barton, S. T. D., L. S. S., Censor
deputatus.
Imprimatur: E. Morrogh Bernard, Vic. Gen.,
Westmonasterii, die 30a Maii 1962
The Nihil obstat and Imprimatur are a declaration that a
book or pamphlet is considered to be free from doctrinal
or moral error. It is not implied that those who have granted
the Nihil obstat and Imprimatur agree with the contents
opinions or statements expressed.

Printed in England

CONTENTS

༄༅

vii

FOREWORD

꿍

THE following pages are a new translation of *Amour et Silence, par un Chartreux,* published by *Les Editions du Seuil* (*la Vigne du Carmel*) in Paris in 1951; and of *La Sainte Trinité et la Vie Surnaturelle* by the same author, published by Egloff of Fribourg and Paris in 1948.

A translation of the first part of *Amour et Silence* was made by Father Michael Day, of the Congregation of the Oratory, and published under the title *The Interior Life* in the Paraclete Series (Cecil Paul Hurwitz, Cork) in 1951, a translation now out of print. Editions have also appeared in Germany, Spain and Italy, and it is thought that a complete translation of this work will be welcomed in the English speaking world. The second work is now translated into English for the first time.

As the author of both works is still living, they are, in accordance with the custom of the Order, published anonymously.

St Hugh's Charterhouse,
Parkminster.
Easter, 1962.

AN INTRODUCTION TO
THE INTERIOR LIFE

INTRODUCTION

လ၁လ၁

OUR Lord tells us that the kingdom of God is within us;[1] and not only within us, but in the very depths of our being. *If any one love me,* he says, *he will keep my word, and my Father will love him; and we will come to him and make our abode with him.*[2]

Unfortunately, we are so apt to forget these truths. There are, of course, many faithful souls who endeavour to lead good lives, and strive to attain to a certain ideal of moral virtue. But how few know how to live a life of real faith, sustained by hope and aflame with the love of God, in order to participate fully in the life that Jesus longs to share with us. We are surrounded and enfolded with the loving care of divine Providence; we have all we need to enter immediately upon a life of the greatest intimacy with God, but we lack the *will* to live the supernatural life. We know the principles: the way lies open before us. If anything prevents us from embarking upon it, then the fault lies in ourselves.

We must admit that *the children of this world are wiser in their generation than the children of light.*[3] We have, indeed, received an infinite treasure, but we do not realize its true worth. And the

[1] Luke xvii, 21.
[2] John xiv, 23.
[3] Luke xvi, 8.

3

very fact of our ignorance of its value prevents us from making the good use of it that we should. Our Lord surely had our heedlessness in mind when he recounted the parable of the wasted talent, which the foolish servant hid, to no purpose, in the ground.[4]

Yet Our Lord has done more than offer us the treasure of his intimate love. He solicits us so insistently that he almost forces us to accept it. He acts towards us in much the same way as we read in the Gospel of the poor wretches who had no alternative but to accept the invitation to the royal banquet: *Compel them to come in.*[5] We hear the same call, and henceforth our prayer will be that of the Church: *Grant unto us, O Lord, an increase of faith, hope and charity.*[6]

But we must not rest content with a few devotional exercises at the beginning and in the course of the day: that does not constitute a *life*. The word *life* denotes a constant, persevering activity: and Our Lord wants to be our life. He said: *I am the Life.*[7] And so we must not only follow in his steps but continue to do so. It is not just this or that particular devotion that he asks of us, but our whole life, our whole strength and our whole soul; so that we may with his help begin, even now, our eternal life. In a word, we must respond to the call of Christ, if we would breathe the pure and radiant air of eternal truth and love.

[4] cf. Matthew xxv, 18.
[5] Luke xiv, 23.
[6] Collect for the 13th Sunday after Pentecost.
[7] John xi, 25.

In order that others may glimpse something of this eternal vision, we propose to outline a simple and straightforward method of meditation, which will enable them to form the habit of turning the whole of their day into a continuous prayer, according to the word of the Gospel: *We ought always to pray, and not to faint.*[8]

But before describing this method, we shall state briefly the principles upon which such a life of prayer is based, and conclude by showing that this teaching, with all it entails, is clearly in accordance with Our Lord's own words in the Gospels.

[8] Luke xviii, 1.

THE PRINCIPLES OF THE
SPIRITUAL LIFE

1. Our Supernatural End

ഗ‍ഗ

Looking back in all sincerity over our spiritual life, we are surprised, if not disheartened, at our slowness, not to say complete lack of progress. How is it that there has been so much effort with so little to show for it? Why, after so many years, it may be, of a life of asceticism, must we own to the same weaknesses, admit the same faults? Is it not possible that from the very beginning we have missed the essential point of it all, and have been following the wrong road?

For there is only one door by which we can enter into our spiritual heritage. In our vain attempts to enter by some other way, it is obvious that we are bound to meet with insuperable difficulties. Have we not been rather like a foolish robber who seeks by some ruse to effect an entrance into a place only too well defended? *He that entereth not by the door, but climbeth up another way*, says Our Lord, *is a thief and a robber.*[1] This one door is Christ: faith in Christ; a faith quickened by love, which by fortifying our heart makes us capable of loving in return with a love which

[1] John x, 1.

7

burns more intensely and radiates more widely, thus resembling more and more the love of Jesus himself.

But first of all we must make one thing perfectly clear. Any kind of asceticism which has for its sole object the perfecting of *self*—an asceticism which is egocentric—is utterly worthless. Such a way of life pays very poor dividends, and the profits it yields are very disappointing. He who sows human seed can only expect to reap a human harvest.

Christian asceticism is based absolutely upon a divine principle, and this same principle inspires and animates it, and guides it to its end. *Thou shalt love the Lord thy God with thy whole heart, and with thy whole soul, and with thy whole strength.*[2] Here we have the summing-up and essence of the Old Law: the New Law has done no more than repeat this first and greatest commandment, making it clearer for all to understand, and promulgating it universally in all its divine simplicity and force. From the very beginning of our spiritual life we must keep our soul set towards this plenitude of love, towards God alone. To act otherwise is to fail to recognize the profound purpose of Christianity; to return to the notion of a self-centred perfection, to that delusive egoism of certain pagan moralists—in a word, to Stoicism, ancient and new—which is so exacting a culture of so miserable a pride.

If only we could convince ourselves once and for all of the truth of the words of our divine

<hr />

[2] Deuteronomy vi, 5.

Master: *Without me, you can do nothing,*[3] how changed our whole outlook would be. If only our minds were penetrated with the doctrine of life contained in those few words, we would concentrate on practising, not just one or two virtues, but all without exception, knowing so well that it is God himself who must be both the term and source of our actions.

Then, having done all we can (as though success depended solely upon our own efforts) we would remain humble in our progress and confident after our falls. Knowing that of ourselves we can do nothing but that in Christ we can do all things, we should no more be discouraged by our faults than proud of the virtuous acts his grace has made possible.

And not only that. Once we are convinced that we are nothing and that God is all, our very weaknesses and failings need no longer be obstacles. Indeed, they are changed into means: they are an occasion for our faith to grow by the exercise of heroic acts, and for our trust to triumph before the manifest rout of all that draws us away from God. *Gladly will I glory in my infirmities,* says the Apostle, *that the power of Christ may dwell in me.*[4]

Once, then, we have learned to trust in God and mistrust our own strength, we shall run like giants in the way of love. More and more will love motivate our actions and purify our intentions, until before long its influence will penetrate every corner of our lives.

[3] John xv, 5.   [4] 2 Corinthians xii, 9.

And so, if we would be faithful to the teaching of the Gospel, we must spare no effort until we have arrived at acting solely from motives of faith and love. And since a purely natural principle can never produce supernatural results, we shall never reach our goal unless from the outset we endeavour to act solely from specifically Christian motives. For if, as St Paul says,[5] we cannot even pronounce Our Lord's name save by his grace, how can we hope, by our own efforts, to arrive at our supernatural end?

We do not deny that, if we are to put our house in order, some effort of will on our part is absolutely necessary; but if we ask ourselves whether the impetus of our will responds more readily and more efficaciously under the influence of faith and grace or when moved solely by reason, we know well the answer. Why not, then, since it is a question of developing our spiritual life, profit as much as we can from the light and strength that the theological virtues can give us? Why not, from the very start, enter straight away into the kingdom within us, into the intimate friendship of God?

This kingdom of Christ lies open before us. Not only so, but it is Our Lord's express desire that we should make that kingdom ours. *Abide in me, and I in you.*[6] Why not respond to his call, and begin to live by faith *now,* even as St Paul tells us: *The just man liveth by faith.*[7]

[5] Corinthians xii, 3.   [6] John xv, 4.
[7] Romans i, 17.

2. THE LIFE OF FAITH

〜〜

WHAT is important above everything else, first
and foremost, is *faith*: faith in the reality of the
divine presence in and around us, bringing the
acts of our will and mind up to the level of the
true life to which Our Lord is calling us. This
act of faith, which transforms our destiny from
a purely human one to one truly divine, is painful
to nature, and calls for a heroism of which we
would not be capable had not God already given
us the grace to make the initial effort and maintain
it. Utterly incapable ourselves of making this first
act, we could not do better than say with the father
of the sick child: *Lord, I do believe; help thou my
unbelief.*[1]

It is faith that gives us the assurance of the divine
promises: *I will espouse thee to me in faith.*[2] It is faith
that makes us walk in its obscurity in this life: *For
we walk by faith.*[3] From start to finish we shall follow
that way, ever on the alert lest we stray from it,
enticed all too readily by lights too human, which
will quickly leave us disillusioned.

Faith is a strict guide but an infallible one. It
knows no concessions, makes no calculations, hesi-
tates before no obstacles. Under the veil of
appearances it discerns even now the eternal truth,
the victory of Christ: *This is the victory which over-
cometh the world, our faith.*[4] It hopes despite all the

[1] Mark ix, 23.   [2] Osee ii, 20.
[3] 2 Corinthians v, 7.   [4] 1 John v, 4.

human factors which seek to moderate or destroy its enthusiasm, even as the Apostle says of Abraham: *He staggered not by distrust, but was strengthened in faith; he hoped against hope.*[5] Faith is at the root of all Our Lord's teaching; to doubt is to grow weak. *O thou of little faith, why didst thou doubt?*[6] By faith we are saved. Our Lord even attributed the miracles he wrought for those he cured, to their faith. One tiny spark of faith is enough to transform spiritually the whole world. *I say to you, if you have faith as a grain of mustard seed . . . nothing shall be impossible to you.*[7]

In short, we must learn to place all our trust in God. These are the words that mark the boundary line which we must cross unhesitatingly and in all simplicity if we would follow Christ.

So, in the few pages which follow, we would indicate the essential lines of the interior life, suggesting a method of meditation at once simple and practical, based on faith. For faith, as we have just shown, is the principle of this life; and when divine grace has finished its work in us, it is this same supernatural certitude which, having filled our whole being, will raise therein a temple of love, according to the words of St Paul: *Faith worketh by charity,*[8] and *Christ will dwell by faith in your hearts, making known to you the superabundant love of God, which surpasseth all knowledge.*[9]

We will now briefly examine the great truths which must serve as a basis for all that follows.

[5] Romans iv, 18–20.
[6] Matthew xiv, 31.
[7] Matthew xvii, 19.
[8] Galatians v, 6.
[9] cf. Ephesians iii, 17–19.

3. God's Natural Presence in all Things

࿇

IN order that we may understand more clearly
God's supernatural presence, let us first of all consider his natural presence in things.

God is everywhere—a simple truth all too easily
forgotten. Yet it is a thought which could change
the whole tenor of our lives.

We tire ourselves at times by trying to imagine
God as someone far away, and our prayer suffers
accordingly. God is a spirit, whose presence is not
limited to any one place but is to be found in all
things. So shall the true adorers of God, we are
told, adore him *in spirit and in truth.*[1] So, too, the
Apostle says: *In him we live and move and have our
being.*[2] This is the first truth that strikes us at the
beginning of our spiritual life, and it would achieve
amazing results if only we could make this thought
of God's actual presence in all things a reality in
our lives.

Even apart from and before all supernatural
revelation, reason tells us that God knows and
sees us completely and constantly, since he knows
and sees all things. *Whither shall I go from thy
spirit, or whither shall I flee from thy face? If I ascend
into heaven, thou art there; if I descend into the abode of
the dead, thou art present.*[3] Not only is God present
to us by simple knowledge, but he governs and
directs us in all our ways. It is he who gives us *both
to will and to accomplish.*[4] Apart from him we cannot

[1] John iv, 23. [2] cf. Acts xvii, 28.
[3] cf. Psalm cxxxviii, 7–8. [4] Philippians ii, 13.

lift a finger. There is nothing, literally nothing, which is not subject to his governance—not even sin. Even when we sin, God is present, since it is he who gives us the power to act and sustains us in the act: the only thing which does not come from him is the depravation of our will. Were we able to do the slightest thing without him, he would not be the first and universal Cause: in other words, he would not be God! *If I take my wings in the morning, and dwell in the uttermost parts of the sea, even there shall thy hand lead me, and thy right hand shall hold me.*[5]

But that is not all. It is not enough that God should watch over us and direct our ways. As the sole and sovereign source of all being he must keep us in existence, giving us at each moment all we are. Were this divine action to cease for one instant, we and the universe itself would vanish like a dream. Once we have understood the necessity for this divine intervention, preserving all that God has created, the tiniest object assumes for us a singular greatness, since it is the omnipotent God and he alone who, present in this little creature, saves it from falling into nothingness.

Who would deny that a shadow is the frailest of realities? Our shadow is nothing compared to ourselves. But compared with God, present within us, we ourselves are even less real: indeed, in the presence of the divine Reality, we are not even shadows!

[5] Psalm cxxxviii, 9–10.

14

4. GOD'S SUPERNATURAL PRESENCE IN THE SOUL

ᔐᔐ

GOD is thus present in this stone and enables it by his direct action to be what it is, namely a stone. But God, in his infinite goodness, wanted to create beings *in his image and likeness*,[1] who, raised to a supernatural state, would resemble him much more than material objects that have only a material being. God is pure spirit. He possesses, therefore, intellect and will, and he has created beings in his likeness who also have intellect and will, to the end that he can be present in them not only as he is in all things but, by raising them to a supernatural state by grace, share with them his own life.

Thus God is present in material things and gives them their being, which is a purely natural being. In creatures endowed with reason, however, he wished, with a generosity entirely gratuitous, to be present in such a way that he not only gives them natural being but also being similar to his own: that is to say, he makes them like himself.

God was not obliged to act thus, but because he is Goodness itself (and all goodness seeks to diffuse itself) he is like a fire which cannot contain itself, but must spread to everything that can burn. *Behold, the Lord thy God is a consuming fire.*[2]

It is this fire which Our Lord came to bring down to the world: *And the Word was made flesh . . .*[3] We know why: *I am come to cast fire on the*

---

[1] Genesis i, 26.   [2] Deuteronomy iv, 24.   [3] John i, 14.

earth, and what will I but that it be kindled.[4] It was to obtain for us the grace to be susceptible to this divine fire that he suffered; and we are susceptible when we have cleared away all obstacles to the divine action. The greatest of these obstacles is sin. *If any one love me,* says Our Lord, *he will keep my word, and we will come to him and will make our abode with him.*[5]

He has done more. He has not only made it possible for us to share in the life of the Father, but he has *desired with desire*[6] to remain among us, and this he accomplished in the Holy Eucharist, and it is in Holy Communion that the divine life in us is increased. *No man cometh to the Father but by me.*[7]

Jesus is the Way—the only way. To want to seek the divine life by any other way is both presumptuous and illusory. The more we are fed with his sacred humanity's love; the more we reflect on the example he has set us, the more will the divine life grow in us. *I am come that they may have life, and may have it more abundantly.*[8]

[4] Luke xii, 49.
[6] cf. Luke xxii, 15.
[8] John x, 10.

[5] John xiv, 23.
[7] John xiv, 6.

5. The Effect of Grave Sin on the Soul

လာလာ

OUR destiny is to a life of the greatest intimacy with God himself. This union between the soul and its Creator was established when God raised our first parents to the supernatural state. But by sin they revolted against God, and the bond between heaven and earth was broken. It needed a man-God to heal that rupture, and it is now, by the Passion and merits of our divine Saviour, that we can once again become children of God, and share in the divine life.

We received that life in baptism and, if it is our misfortune to have forfeited that life by sin, Our Lord gives it back to us through the merits of his Precious Blood every time we receive absolution.

Now we realize how absolutely essential it is for us to avoid sin if we are to preserve the most precious gift God has given to man. *If thou didst know the gift of God* . . .[1] God grant that Our Lord's words to the woman at the well may never become a reproach to us.

All the evils in the world are nothing compared to one sin, for one grave sin robs us of the divine life. In order to understand something of the gravity of sin, think of what it means. What Christian would dare to enter a church furtively and violate the Tabernacle, scattering the sacred Hosts from the dishonoured ciborium? Even if we thought of such a thing, would we have the

[1] John iv, 10.

unhappy daring to do it? Surely, even the most lukewarm Christian would not dare to commit such a sacrilege to the Body of Our Lord. Yet what does sin in fact do? Does it not banish God from our hearts, and deliver us over to the power of Satan?

6. How God is Supernaturally Present in Us

∽∽

WE know that God is one in nature and three in Persons. The Father from all eternity begets the Son, his 'other self', his perfect image. This is not something that took place long ago: it takes place in an eternal present, in an eternal now. The Father is perpetually begetting the Son. And the Father looks upon the Son, divine and co-eternal and, in this loving gaze that they exchange in the simplicity of the divine Essence, they breathe forth the Holy Spirit.

This divine life which will be the substance of our eternal happiness has already begun in the soul, so long as we are in a state of grace. At every moment the Father is begetting the Son within us, and at every moment they together breathe forth in us the Holy Spirit. Have we given sufficient thought to this sublime truth?

We carry about with us scapulars, medals, relics and so on, and we think—and rightly so—that we possess something wonderful. Yet all the while we bear within us the living God, heaven itself, the unique desire of all; the supreme Reality: and we give it not so much as a thought! We would not dream of going out without a rosary in our pocket and we forget all about the Holy of Holies that we carry within us. We are 'other Christophers': Christ-bearers in the strictest sense of the word. Well may we remember the saying of St Leo: *O Christian, remember thy dignity.*[1]

From these very simple reflections we may draw one important conclusion. Is it not obvious that if this divine indwelling, this presence of God within us, influenced our lives as it should do, how utterly changed and transformed our lives would become.

[1] St Leo the Great: *serm. xxi, 3.*

7. LIVING IN THAT PRESENCE

∾

H o w are we to arrive at so obvious an ideal?

God would not be infinite Goodness and
Wisdom if, seeking and even demanding our love,
he had not at the same time made it possible for
us to enter into this intimacy with himself. The
means he has provided, and of which we can be
absolutely certain, to enter into immediate contact
with him, are the theological virtues and the gifts
which accompany them.

By faith we adhere to the truth of the divine life
offered to us. By charity this life becomes ours. By
hope we are certain, with the help of grace, to live
this life more and more, and finally to possess it
for ever in eternity.

This is the essence of all true and real prayer.
Instead of frittering away our time of prayer on
various points; instead of philosophizing *about* God,
multiplying acts of the intellect, of the will and the
imagination, in order to conjure up 'pictures' of
what we are thinking about, how much simpler it
is to go to God directly in our hearts. *Seek him in
simplicity of heart.*[1] It is Our Lord himself who gives
us the invitation. *Be ye simple as doves.*[2] Man is a
complex being, but it would be a pity if he intro-
duced his complications into his relations with
God. God, on the contrary, is simplicity itself. The
more complicated we are, therefore, the farther we

[1] Wisdom i, 1.
[2] Matthew x, 16.

21

stray from him; the simpler we are, on the other hand, the closer we come to him.

We have seen that God, our Father, is present in us. When a child wants to talk to his father he does not make use of a manual of etiquette or a code of manners: he speaks in a simple and unaffected way, without formality; and we must do the same with our heavenly Father. He himself said: *Unless you become as little children, you shall not enter into the kingdom of heaven.*[3] A mother never grows tired of hearing her little one say: 'Mother, I love you'. It is the same with God. The more childlike our prayer, the more it is pleasing to him. After all it was he who chose for himself the name of *Father.* It is the Holy Spirit who cries in us: *Abba, Pater.*[4] It is the Holy Spirit also who places on our lips the inspired words of Scripture and of other liturgical texts.

Our prayer, then, must be quite simple—as simple as possible. All we have to do is to place ourselves on our knees, and with complete sincerity make our acts of faith, hope and love. There is no method of prayer more certain, more elevated, and more salutary than this.

[3] Matthew xviii, 3.
[4] Galatians iv, 6.

A METHOD OF PRAYER

Acts of Faith, Hope and Love

∽∽

Faith
MY God, I believe that you are present in me, even though I am nothing. Indeed I am less than nothing, since I have offended you and rebelled against you. The very beasts of the field have not dishonoured you as I have done, and yet you still want to dwell in me. I ought to be bowed down with shame, instead of which I am prouder than ever and filled with self-love. Nevertheless, my God, in spite of everything I adore you present in my soul. I firmly believe that you are present within me, and with the help of your grace I will try to grow so strong in faith that nothing will draw me away from you. Like the blind man in the Gospel I will say: *Lord, that I may see.*[1] Remove the scales from my eyes, cure my blindness, and may I be so dazzled by the light of your presence that I may see you in all things and all things in you.

Hope
My God, I hope in you who in your infinite goodness have longed to dwell in my heart. But how

[1] Mark x, 51.

23

can I, a most wretched and ungrateful sinner,
dare to hope? Ought I not rather to say with St
Peter: *Depart from me, O Lord, for I am a sinful
man.*[2]

Yet I know that you came on earth, not for the
just who have no need of a Saviour but for sinners
such as I. It is thus that I dare to approach you,
and it is because I am a sinner that I dare to hope
in you.

Nor am I content with mere hope; for I have the
certitude that you are with me and within me, and
that you always will be. As St Paul says: *If God be for
us, who is against us . . . For I am sure that neither
death nor life, nor any creature shall be able to separate
us from the love of God, which is in Christ Jesus.*[3] Henceforth, my God, I know that I can trust you, and I
will fear nothing. Even should the world, the flesh
and the devil combine against me, I shall still not
be afraid, for you are by my side, my Emmanuel,
God with us, my God and my All!

Love

My God, dare I say that I love you; I who have
offended you so often? If I think of my life as a
line, it should be a straight and continous line of
pure love for you, since you created me to love
you. Instead, I see little bits here and there when,
it is true, I have loved you. But even when my
actions have been most generous and my intentions most pure, they have been spoilt by vanity

[2] Luke v, 8.
[3] Romans viii, 31, 38–39.

24

and self-love. In return for your love I have given you only ingratitude.

But here and now, my God, I turn to you, and now it is my turn to say: 'Lord, you have conquered. You died for love of me, I will try to live for love of you. And if I cannot say that I love you, at least I can say that I want to!'

In proposing the above acts we are not suggesting that we should confine ourselves to these alone. There are other acts, for example, of humility, trust, abandonment, adoration and so on: anything, in short, that will help us to acquire real virtue and overcome our faults. What is certain is that it is quite impossible to form a habit of speaking to God in all simplicity in the way we have suggested without making real progress in our spiritual life. Provided we are in good dispositions and that our prayer arises out of the fulness of our heart, there is no reason why we should not pass the time of our meditation in making such acts. On the contrary, we will have made a very good meditation.

Should we find ourselves, however, high and dry and, after making our acts of faith and so on, at the end of our tether, it would be as well to fall back on a sentence or two out of a book, as a subject of conversation with Our Lord. In order to do this to good purpose, however, it is not enough to skim through page after page: we should stop at each sentence and try to make it as vivid and as personal as we can—make it 'ours' in other words, speaking to Our Lord thus: 'You are my God, and I am your creature'.

We read, for instance, some such sentence as: 'And Jesus suffered for men', and immediately we make it: 'My God, it was for *me* you suffered'; and thus it becomes not just a general abstract thought but something personal to ourselves, and we find ourselves saying to Our Lord: 'My God, how burning must be your love for us; who are you that you should have come down from heaven? Why did you do it, and what made you suffer so? . . . Was it for me?'

And then the thought comes to us: 'It was *in order* to suffer that you became man—to suffer immeasurably—*for me,* an ungrateful sinner. It was I who helped to put you to death, and yet you prayed for such as me. And I? I cannot even bear the slightest contradiction, although I know I deserve to suffer far more than this. . . . No longer can I remain indifferent to your cry ever in my ears: *I thirst!*[4] It is true, you suffered actual physical thirst because of my sins; but your real thirst was for the love I have failed to give you. From now on, dear Lord, I will give you my love, and always my love. All that I do henceforth will be in union with your love, and for love of you!'

[4] John xix, 28.

2. THE USE OF THE IMAGINATION

ოო

SOME may object that this method of prayer calls for too little use of the imagination. All the same, it is our opinion that the imagination should be used only when it is strictly necessary; for it is a purely human function and its use is not therefore substantially *prayer*. This alone is one reason why it should be kept within bounds.

Any purely human faculty, under the influence of grace, can be raised and used for a supernatural end; but the fact remains that the imagination, like all sense activity, is quickly exhausted and soon tires of its object. To form and keep before one's mind imaginary pictures is very fatiguing, and it is impossible to keep it up for long. We must, therefore, avoid allowing it to play an important or essential part in our prayer. If we are to obey the Gospel command, our prayer must be simple and continuous.

Nor for that matter can the imagination touch supernatural truths, which can only be apprehended by pure faith. All it can do is to play with the shadows of these realities, which are invisible and can only be the object of the theological virtues. Does that mean that we must banish all images from our prayer? That is not possible. But we do suggest that they should be resorted to only when necessary and not otherwise.

If we are thinking of meditating on the Passion of Our Lord, it is as present in our souls that we must first think of him. Then, with the help of a

crucifix for example, we may, by using our imagination, dwell upon all he suffered for us upon the
Cross. But all the time we must never lose sight of
the fact that Jesus is in our heart. This will not in
any way affect the ardour or strength of our feelings
of compassion for Our Lord. On the contrary, it is
pure faith which gives these feelings their reality
and depth; which assures us that just as our sins
really made Our Lord suffer in his Passion, so our
acts of love have really consoled him. What an
encouragement for a fervent soul to know that it
can now, by its love, console Jesus alone in his
agony in the Garden of Gethsemane. And this is
not just imagination: it is the sublime reality of
faith.

3. The Conclusion of our Prayer

THE conclusion that we should always draw from our meditations and from our spiritual reading is this: GOD IS ALL, and we are nothing. Thus: 'My God, you are infinite Being, and I am nothing. You are Beauty, and I all sordidness and misery. You are sanctity, and I sin.' And so, little by little, we arrive at an abiding sorrow for sin, which is the basis of all serious interior life. We shall realize, finally, that we are totally incapable of any good, and that the only way for us to *live* is to let God live in us—giving place to his presence, his intentions, his grace.

The resolution that we should make at the conclusion of our prayer should be: to keep ourselves as far as we can, during the rest of the day, in the presence of God, withdrawing from time to to time within ourselves in order to adore him there by acts of faith, hope and love. By these means we will be able to avoid sin, and advance steadily in virtue.

4. THE SPIRIT OF PRAYER

∽∾

BY thus repeating during the day our morning
acts of faith, hope and love, we shall develop in
us the spirit of prayer. The word of St John will
become a guiding star in our lives: *God is Love;
and he that abideth in love abideth in God and
God in him.*[1] And gradually we will come to
realize those other words of the same Apostle:
*Whosoever is born of God committeth not
sin.*[2]

It should not be difficult to withdraw from time
to time from our ordinary preoccupations during
the day to lift up our hearts to God, in accordance
with the Psalmist's words: *It is good for me to
adhere to my God.*[3] I can always turn to him, and
it is not even necessary to express my thoughts in
words. An inward glance, an aspiration, is sufficient. And so gradually I will create for myself
an interior solitude, where I can always listen to
the voice of the Beloved, as he himself said: *I will
lead her into a place apart, and will speak to her
heart.*[4] And thus I will strive always more and
more faithfully to listen to his voice speaking to
me: *I will hear what the Lord God will speak in me.*[5]
When difficulties arise I will take refuge near him:
he will be my Light, and with him I will share my
joys. In a word, it is he who will hold the first place
in my heart and be the object of my actions. My

[1] 1 John iv, 16.   [2] 1 John iii, 9.
[3] Psalm lxxii, 28.   [4] cf. Osee ii, 14.
[5] Psalm lxxxiv, 9.

life, hitherto centred around myself, will find its centre in God alone.

All this I will do without violence, without any kind of strain. The repetition of supernatural acts increasingly disposes one for supernatural habits. If I want, therefore, to arrive at a life lived continuously in an atmosphere of faith, hope and love, I have only to multiply these same acts. Knowing without the slightest doubt that God is calling me to the intimacy of his love, I will spare no pains to 'run in the way of the commandments'.[6] *My delights are to be with the children of men.*[7]

[6] cf. Psalm cxviii, 32.
[7] Proverbs viii, 31.

5. The Life of Prayer: Its Purpose and End

∽∽

AT last, I have found my ideal. Now I know where I want to go, where I can go, and that I shall arrive at my goal. Hitherto, I have groped my way in the darkness; the difficulties I have encountered have wearied and discouraged me. *Now I know,*[1] and henceforth nothing will hold me back. I will not rest until I have found God in the innermost depths of my heart: *I have found him whom my soul loveth: I held him, and I will not let him go.*[2] Love will give me wings, for *love is strong as death.*[3] Difficulties will no longer matter, for *I can do all things in him who strengtheneth me.*[4]

If I glance over my past life and am truly sincere with myself, I will have to admit that so far my spiritual life has lacked an ideal, and that is the real reason I have made so little progress. I have failed to understand how deeply God loves and seeks souls: souls that will give themselves to him so that he may give himself to them. The degree of intimacy to which Our Lord calls us will be achieved in the measure of the generosity of our response to grace. His love is without measure, and longs to give itself completely to souls. But souls are afraid, because of the consequences of that intimacy which calls for great sacrifices on our part.

In future, however, I shall be honest with myself.

---

[1] cf. 2 Timothy i, 12.   [2] Canticle of Canticles iii, 4.
[3] Canticle of Canticles viii, 6.   [4] Philippians iv, 13.

On the one hand, I know that God wants to take full and entire possession of my soul and that he has predestined me to be *conformable to the image of his Son.*[5] He wants me to be his son by adoption. On the other hand, I know also that my unworthiness is no obstacle to his love. Who, indeed, could deem himself worthy? *If we say that we have no sin, we deceive ourselves.*[6]

But there is much more than this. It is not in spite of our unworthiness that God seeks our love, but *because* of it: that he may reveal his glory in us. The more unworthy the material, the more is glory reflected on an artist who can fashion a master-piece out of it. It is this truth that Our Lord tried to bring home to men in the parables of the prodigal son, and of the lost sheep.[7] There is more joy in heaven, we are told, over one sinner doing penance than over all the just.[8] If, then, I have made up my mind to persevere in my ideal, I must be continually acknowledging that, on the one hand, I am nothing and can do nothing of myself, but that, on the other hand, God is all: that he can do all things and wants to do all in me, so that I can make a complete oblation of my life to him.

[5] Romans viii, 29. [6] 1 John i, 8.
[7] cf. Luke xv, 4 and 11. [8] Luke xv, 7.

6. Obstacles Become Means

～い～

ALL that I have hitherto thought of as difficulties—
temptations, distractions, trials, both interior and
exterior—from now onwards will become means.
Up to now all these things have held me back,
leaving me discouraged, but from now on they are
all going to serve as stepping-stones to bring me
nearer to God by detaching me from creatures. I
shall see in them only God's pressing invitation to
unite myself still further to him by acts of faith,
trust, abandonment and love. What has hitherto
been painful to nature now becomes a grace,
forcing me out of myself so that I may live only in
God.

If, so far, I have allowed myself to be too busy or
pre-occupied to do much with my life, now I shall
live in a spirit of confidence and abandonment to
divine Providence. Hitherto my falls and failures
have worried me, but now I shall glory in them.
Gladly, therefore, says St Paul, *will I glory in my infirmities, that the power of Christ may dwell in me.*[1] They
will be the means whereby Christ will live in me.
The secret is always the same: to grow in ever closer
union with God by means of the theological virtues
at the expense of the natural man. *Christ must
increase, but I must decrease,*[2] and he increases in the
measure in which I decrease.

And so, little by little, I will learn to dominate
contingent things, and my enemies of yesterday

[1] Corinthians xii, 9.   [2] cf. John iii, 30.

34

will become my soul's friends of today, actually
aiding me in my progress towards my ideal. More
and more will I place all my faculties and all my
being at the disposal of God. More and more
clearly will I hear his voice speaking in my soul.
And thus I trust the day will come when, by an
unspeakable grace, my soul will really be one with
him. *My soul melted when he spoke*, says the bride in
the Canticle of Canticles.[3] Nor will I rest until I
have arrived at this haven of my delight, which is
ever before my eyes. For every lost moment I will
make reparation by an increase of fervour, and
thus will my faith grow stronger, my hope surer,
and my love more intense.

[3] Canticle of Canticles v, 6.

7. The Application of These Principles to Everyday Life

✍

And now I ask myself the question: how can I apply these principles of my meditation so that my whole life becomes a life of prayer?

Before engaging in any activity, and from time to time during the course of it, I must stop for a moment and glance inwardly at the divine Guest within my soul. I can do this by choosing any words I am in the habit of repeating, such as the opening words of the Divine Office, or the *Gloria Patri* when reciting the rosary. By these repeated acts of recollection, I will gradually form a habit of living in that sacred presence, until the time will come when I am never separated from it.

So, too, my evening examination of conscience will consist of quietly going over the events of the day to see whether, through any fault of mine, I have forgotten Our Lord for too long. And I will notice that it is just in these moments of forgetfulness that I fall into temptation.

Again: when engaged in spiritual or any other kind of reading it is as well to stop, even if it is only when turning over the page, and withdraw myself and thus renew my contact with God within me. The same applies to times of relaxation or when out walking. In other words, I should never entirely lose sight of my inner life but, by simple aspirations, renew my interior union with God, resting in his sacred intimacy, conscious that I am surrounded by his love. I will treat him as a very dear Friend: there will be no need to exchange many words; it is enough to know and feel that he is by my side. Sometimes I shall find myself in places and surroundings where he is forgotten, and then I will make my acts of love more fervent than ever.

Then, while grace is doing its work in me, I on my part will do all I can by such ordinary means that are at my disposal to develop the divine life within me. I can do this by spiritual reading, study and so on; and by these means deepen my appreciation of the Church's teaching, especially in all that concerns the doctrine of our adoption by grace as sons of God.

And, finally and above all, I shall frequent the sacraments as often as I can, and with all the fervour of which I am capable; for they are the surest channels of grace. Indeed it is through the sacred humanity of Christ that we approach his divinity. *No man*, Our Lord said, *cometh to the Father but by me:*[1] that is, through the Incarnate Son of God.

In a mysterious way, he purifies us in giving us absolution. Through the Holy Eucharist, by nourishing us with his humanity, he makes us enter ever deeper into his divinity. Even after the sacramental species have ceased to be present in us, we are still *partakers of the divine nature.*[2] Nor need we think that our thanksgiving is limited to a quarter of an hour or so. Like the

[1] John xiv, 6.
[2] cf. 2 Peter i, 4.

disciples who met Our Lord on the way to Emmaus, our prayer will be: *Stay with us, Lord.*[3] And so Holy Communion becomes the inexhaustible source upon which our inner life feeds, its action spreading over the whole day, and constantly renewing our fervour.

Let us place ourselves entirely in the hands of Our Blessed Lady. She will give birth in us to her Son, and will watch over his growth until we are *made perfect in one.*[4]

[3] Luke xxiv, 29.
[4] John xvii, 23.

THE GOSPEL BASIS

WE are not suggesting that there is anything new in the method of prayer which we have outlined in the foregoing pages. On the contrary, anyone reading the Gospels will at once see that it is all contained in Our Lord's own words.

When spiritual writers treat of the Christian way of life in general, and of the interior life in particular, they usually stress our duties and obligations. They rarely tell us of the treasures of beauty and joy that God has in store, even in this life, for the faithful soul. What we already *possess* in the supernatural order seems to be forgotten in the anxiety of stressing what we have to *give.* What God asks of us, that is to say our possessions and ourselves, is nothing compared to what he promises us in return, namely himself and an eternity of infinite happiness. This divine exchange is made abundantly clear in the Gospels, but so many writers misrepresent our relations with God by failing to remind us of these spiritual joys which are ours now, through the generosity of our divine Lord.

39

1. THE EVANGELICAL COUNSELS

∽∽

PERFECT union with God can only come to us by way of some form of death to self. Already the Old Testament foreshadowed this when God said: *No man shall see me and live.*[1] Our Lord, too, is terribly insistent upon this point. He asks of us a total sacrifice that no merely human wisdom would dare to impose: *Unless you shall do penance, you shall all likewise perish.*[2] And: *If any man will come after me, let him deny himself, and take up his cross daily and follow me.*[3] *He that hateth not his father and mother . . . yea, and his own life also, cannot be my disciple.*[4] The most rigorous maxims of the ascetical life are merely repetitions of these truths, though rarely do they dare to reproduce the severity of Our Lord's words. Yet, if we would follow Christ, we must immolate our whole self, keeping back absolutely nothing not even in thought. For *God hateth rapine in the holocaust.*[5] And Jesus said: *No man putting his hand to the plough and looking back is fit for the kingdom of God.*[6] And: *Because thou art lukewarm, I will vomit thee out of my mouth.*[7]

[1] cf. Exodus xxxiii, 20.
[2] Luke xiii, 3.
[3] Luke ix, 23.
[4] cf. Luke xiv, 26.
[5] cf. Isaias lxi, 8.
[6] Luke ix, 62.
[7] Apocalypse iii, 16.

2. OUR LORD'S LAST WORDS

THE precepts and counsels which urge us so repeatedly to die to ourselves represent only the negative side of Christ's teaching. If we would know his mind fully in this matter, we must read and re-read above all the fourth Gospel. For in the synoptic Gospels Our Lord speaks mostly in parables. It is in St John's Gospel that he reveals explicitly the plan of his love, and tells us clearly why he is so stern in asking for the sacrifice of our poor life. *It is in order that he may give us his own in return.* We cannot read and ponder on these pages too often, for they are in effect Our Lord's spiritual testament. Compared to his burning words, the counsels of spiritual writers in general pale into insignificance. Of all books on the ascetical life the Gospel is by far the severest and most exacting. But it is also more authoritative and daring and more generous in its call to the supernatural life, and in its promise of a life of intimacy with God, than any work on mystical prayer.

In these chapters of St John's Gospel,[1] Our Lord tells us that he intends to make known to us the supreme secret of his teaching. He will no longer speak in parables. *Behold, now thou speakest plainly, and speakest no proverb.*[2] His discourse after the Last Supper and his Sacerdotal Prayer are a summing-up of and at the same time

---

[1] John xiv–xvii.   [2] cf. John xvi, 29.

41

the key to the whole of his teaching. The need for penance and mortification is indicated in a few verses, which recall the theme developed by the other Evangelists. There is no love, he tells us, without fidelity to the precepts: *If you love me, keep my commandments.*[3] We cannot follow Christ and be his friend without taking up our cross: *He that hath my commandments and keepeth them, he it is that loveth me.*[4] *You are my friends if you do the things that I command you.*[5] Obedience to the commandments is the sign by which we will recognize his disciples in the midst of the world. One of his disciples said to him: *Lord, how is it that thou wilt manifest thyself to us, and not to the world?* And Jesus answered: *If any one love me, he will keep my word.*[6] And it is by this word that the world is condemned.

Our Lord did not hide from the apostles the sufferings and contradictions they would have to face in leaving all things and following him. On the contrary, he said: *If you had been of the world, the world would love its own; but because you are not of the world . . . therefore the world hateth you.*[7] *I have given them thy word, and the world hath hated them; because they are not of the world, even as I also am not of the world.*[8] *You shall lament and weep, but the world shall rejoice.*[9] *In the world you shall have many tribulations, but have confidence: I have overcome the world.*[10]

[3] John xiv, 15.
[5] John xv, 14.
[7] John xv, 19.
[9] John xvi, 20.

[4] John xiv, 21.
[6] John xiv, 22–23.
[8] John xvii, 14.
[10] cf. John xvi, 33.

3. HIS PROMISES

∽∽

OBEDIENCE and patience, we must remember, are not ends in themselves. 'Art for art's sake' is nonsense, since nothing created can be its own end. It is the same with virtue. 'Virtue for virtue's sake' as an ideal is meaningless and discouraging, because it can never be realized. Anyone leaving the world for the paltry pleasure of thinking himself perfect, or who accepts the world's challenge from a sense of spiritual pride or to increase his self-esteem, is simply ending up where he began—with himself! When Our Lord asks us to empty our hearts, it is because he wants to fill them with his own love. And it is only when he does fill our hearts that the work of our purification has achieved its object. In the same way, the divine life can only take possession of us when we have done all we can, on our part, to become detached from created things. Death to self and life in God are inseparably linked: the one without the other remains sterile.

Listen to Our Lord's promises to those who keep his word: promises that he longs with divine impatience to realize in us. *He that loveth me shall be loved of my Father, and I will love him and will manifest myself to him; and we will come to him, and will make our abode with him. In that day, you shall know that I am in my Father, and you in me, and I in you. . . . And I will ask the Father, and he shall give you another Paraclete, that he may abide with you for ever . . .*

43

the Spirit of Truth. He shall abide with you, and shall be in you.[1]

This mutual inhabitation, this indwelling, this amazing intimacy with the three divine Persons, is the ultimate goal that souls must have in view from the very outset of their spiritual life. Such is the wish and will of our divine Saviour. It is not enough to persuade souls to tend *towards* a heavenly ideal; they must be made to enter *into* the kingdom of God, and made to understand that it is already their inheritance. *The kingdom of God is within you.*[2]

Apart from that life of union with Our Lord, with the companionship of the Father and of the Holy Spirit which follows from that union, there can be no real or deep spiritual life, nor any true spiritual progress. *Abide in me,* said Our Lord, *and I in you. As the branch cannot bear fruit of itself unless it abide in the vine, so neither can you unless you abide in me. . . . He that abideth in me and I in him, the same beareth much fruit; for without me you can do nothing.*[3]

If anyone abide not in me, he shall be cast forth as a branch and shall wither; and they shall gather him up and cast him into the fire . . . If you abide in me, you shall ask whatever you will, and it shall be done unto you. In this is my Father glorified.[4]

No one can have any conception of the power of the silent prayer of such a soul united to our divine Lord. *In that day,* says Our Lord, *you shall*

[1] John xiv, 16 ff.   [2] Luke xvii, 21.
[3] John xv, 4–5.   [4] John xv, 6–8.

44

not ask me anything... If you ask the Father anything in my name, he will give it you.[5] *I say not to you that I will ask the Father for you; for the Father himself loveth you, because you have loved me and have believed that I came out from God.*[6]

If we listen, thus, to the divine voice and 'ponder these things in our heart' as Our Lady did, like her we shall become each a 'seat of wisdom'. For Our Lord has explicitly promised to those in whom he with his Father and the Holy Spirit would dwell, a gift of which the world knows nothing. *The Paraclete, the Holy Ghost, will teach you all things, and bring all things to your mind whatsoever I have said to you.*[7] *I will not now call you servants, for the servant knoweth not what his Lord doth. But I will call you friends, because all things whatsoever I have heard of my Father I have made known to you.*[8] *When he, the Spirit of Truth, is come, he will teach you all truth.*[9]

This knowledge that will be given to us is of our eternal life—the life which has already begun in our souls. *Now this is eternal life: that they may know thee, the only true God, and Jesus Christ whom thou hast sent.*[10] It is not just an abstract and theoretical knowledge but a wisdom lived, full of love, radiating charity, mercy and kindness. This torrent of divine love overwhelms the obedient and faithful soul, spreading far and wide,

[5] John xvi, 23.
[6] John xvi, 26–27.
[7] John xiv, 26.
[8] John xv, 15.
[9] John xvi, 13.
[10] John xvii, 3.

45

until it rises up again to return to its Source. In the measure in which the love becomes more generous and more intense will the soul be enriched with a deeper knowledge, thus giving birth to an ever increasing love. *Abide in my love*[11] ... *He that loveth me shall be loved of my Father, and I will love him, and will manifest myself to him.*[12]

When the mind and will have thus been purified and led back to their Source; when the soul is drawn into the stream of the divine life, then at last will it know true joy. *These things I have spoken to you that my joy may be in you, and your joy may be filled.*[13] *Your sorrow shall be turned into joy, that no man shall take from you.*[14] *These things I have spoken to you that in me you may have peace.*[15] *Peace I leave with you, my peace I give unto you.*[16]

In the limpid simplicity and deep security of a life divinized to its very depths, the soul at last rejoices to hear within those depths the concluding words of Our Lord's prayer: *That they all may be one, as thou Father in me and I in thee: that they also may be one in us ... And the glory which thou hast given me I have given to them ... that they may be made perfect in one; and the world may know that thou hast sent me and hast loved them, as thou hast also loved me.*[17]

[11] John xv, 9.
[12] John xiv, 21.
[13] John xv, 11.
[14] John xvi, 20–22.
[15] John xvi, 33.
[16] John xiv, 27.
[17] John xvii, 21–23.

SERMONS IN CHAPTER

EPIPHANY

෴

*I am come that they may have life,
and may have it more abundantly*
John x, 10

THE birth of Our Lord is a renewal of creation.
The Fathers of the Church have compared the
Infant-God, hidden under the triple veil of the
maternal womb, of a cave and of night, to the
secret seed whence a new Flower will blossom
for the joy of the world. All life, it so happens,
is born in secret and is veiled in its beginnings
with mystery and silence. And Our Lord is
Life itself: *Ego sum vita . . . I am Life.*[1] We
shall never meditate enough on this name,
so rich in its meaning, that God has given to
himself.

The life he communicates to us is not the life of
nature but of grace. Nevertheless, the first is the
figure of the second, and the latter the fulness of
the former. All life is freely given. In a living
person life is the first and fundamental gift for
which there can be neither preparation nor merit.
It is not for nothing that the supernatural life is
called grace, for it is life essential: a birth more
mysterious, a gift more pure and unmerited, than
that of nature, for it is a participation in the

[1] John xiv, 6.

49

divine prerogatives that no created intelligence would have thought possible. We must possess the spirit of grace, the spirit of divine liberality which, when we receive God's gifts, makes us welcome without hesitation all that he offers us so lavishly, and when we give, constrains us by a consummate generosity to imitate the divine abundance of that living water, sharing it with others, whilst we ourselves drink deeply of the source.

Among the faithful generally, it is by prayer and recollection that grace is diffused. With us, it must do so above all under the form of the interior life. Interiorness is a characteristic of all life. An inanimate stone has a kind of activity, but it is only on the surface; it only resists shocks from without. Living things, on the other hand, discern and utilize whatever is good for them: an inner sense guides their conduct and growth. The spiritual life is even keener and more powerful still: there is nothing from which it cannot draw profit. The faithful soul finds its good in everything that affects it; a principle more profound than that which governs the life of nature causes it to derive strength and development from its contact with everything. When it is not so with us, when we allow the accidents of life to upset us and turn us from our path, it is surely because our life is not sufficiently interior. We must descend into the depths of our being, remain patient and still and re-find in the solitude where God dwells that divine intelligence, that mysterious force, thanks to which we are again able to assimilate harmoniously without exception all that happens to us and around us.

As for us, the life of grace, the interior life, is developed under the form of the contemplative life. Perhaps, in order to make this union and fusion of man with his Creator clearer we should express ourselves more simply, and it would be truer to say in general that we lead a life of union and love. None the less, we rightly speak of it as the contemplative life to denote the ideal of a love essentially direct and disinterested. For contemplation is the act of a soul rapt in admiration in the presence of something more beautiful than itself. (Such, indeed, is the nature of admiration, the force of beauty thus contemplated, that it can make us 'lose ourselves', utterly unconscious of our 'self'). The act of contemplative love is at once the simplest and most direct. Here again we cannot help remarking the continuity of the processes of nature and grace. All life is love, and all life is forgetfulness of self. Life consists in losing oneself so as to gain a higher good. In all nature life can only be perpetuated by the immolation of the individual, sacrificed generation after generation, so that the flame of life it has received may be passed on and continue, undiminished, a living flame.

But it is, above all, in the realm of grace that that abnegation is both a necessity and a joy. *Qui perdiderit animam suam* . . . *he that shall lose his life for me shall find it.*[2] The soul has the

---

[2] Matthew x, 39.

power to forget itself more than any other living thing; it has, if it so desire, the absolute limpidity of a mirror. Possessing no longer any form of its own, it reflects all the splendour of the infinite Majesty. To contemplate God thus, in the calm of recollection, is the source of all true wisdom. We are not masters of ourselves, we shall never know true justice or prudence, until by a brave and sincere gesture of welcome we allow God to fulfil his will in us, and be in us all he wants to be.

May Mary, whose feast it is also today, Mary full of grace, the most interior and hidden of virgins, whose soul is lost in pure admiration of the divine Majesty and thus utterly free, teach us to receive him, and to love and contemplate him, as she herself does.

EPIPHANY (2)

ᗢᗢ

I would like to examine with you today a question which interests all solitaries, namely the struggle we all have against obsessions.

An obsession is an idea or image which takes up undue room in our thoughts, when it should only play a very modest role, or better still none at all. Such are the obsessions one meets with most frequently in the consciences of religious. We imagine we are hated or persecuted. We are jealous or rebellious in face of a superiority, real or imagined, on the part of one of our brethren. We harbour wearying fears for our own health or for the well-being, physical or otherwise, of our family. We are roused to impatience at the imperfections of others. We are worked up all to no purpose by assuming the role of mentor for the good of others who are not under us nor subject to our jurisdiction or authority. These are only a few examples, but the direction and forms our obsessions take are infinite.

The proper way to suppress these disorders is to endeavour to restore that right judgment which is lacking. An obsession normally is due, in great part if not altogether, to the fact that we do not see things as they are. It arises from a false idea which imposes itself in such a way that it upsets the normal trend of our thoughts. The best remedy, of course, would be to recognize quite simply that the idea we have is not true, and so put matters right. Unhappily, where the faculty for forming judgments is defective, there is no natural or direct way of correcting it. However, by trying to remain calm and by taking the necessary time to think things over quietly—above all, by remaining recollected in God's presence—we can create conditions more favourable to the exercise of a right judgment. Further, there is one virtue which is the enemy of all foolishness, and that is humility. Anyone who is humble is invariably sensible in essentials, for he knows his proper place. And when we are in our place (which is the last[1]), we see things in their true light. Anyone who is not able to think clearly and does not mind acknowledging it will, if he will submit his judgment to a director (even if *his* judgment is not exceptional), by the very fact be delivered from many scruples and foolish thoughts with which another would be obsessed. Be modest, open and docile—these are the three great remedies against all false ideas. Otherwise their importunity will risk making our life as solitaries very unhappy as well as robbing it of its dignity.

There is no question that in the choice of candidates for a solitary life such as ours, an open mind and sound commonsense are absolutely essential. Some people are astonished at this insistence; there is no need, they say, for all this judgment in order to leave the world. But they are wrong. In order to free oneself and become detached from things, one must see them in their true perspective, value them at their true worth,

[1] cf. Luke xiv, 10.

and give them their proper due. One needs as much judgment to renounce the things of the world as to acquire and keep possession of them— more in fact!

At other times, however, it is not enough to bring to bear a right judgment in order to rid ourselves of an obsession which can, after all, have some foundation in fact. I may be obsessed by an imaginary illness, or by the idea of persecution; but it can be that I am really ill, and really persecuted. In such cases, it is not the idea of tyranny which is, strictly speaking, false but the importance that it assumes in our interior life. There are times when we know definitely by the light of faith that the thing or person whose image or thought is haunting us is not worth the anxiety it is causing us, and yet we are still obsessed by it. In such cases, we must remember that the will of a Christian is given him to come to the support of his judgment and in some ways to complete it. It has to impose its spiritual certitudes on the imagination and on one's sensitive nature. We may know certain things to be true, but we still need to make their truth felt in the lower part of the soul; and for that we must make a continuous effort to be recollected and to keep a grip on ourselves, which is one of the essential elements of the Christian life. It is a struggle we cannot avoid. The most we can do, as we know from experience, is to learn how to wage this spiritual warfare.

It is true there are physical conditions that make things difficult, and to know how to keep oneself in hand wisely is half the battle. Here, however, we would confine ourselves to spiritual means. From that point of view, all obsessions have as cause a certain resistance on the part of our self-love. We do not *want* to accept our share of suffering and humiliations. So we must once and for all consent to allow ourselves to be put on one side, to abandon ourselves. It is often a mere thread that attaches us to our unhappiness, but we hold the end of it and will not let it go. To give God all he asks for, totally and absolutely with an unreserved *Amen*, is the only way to rid ourselves of these miseries. There is a proverb which says: *Where there is nothing, a king has no rights.* For anyone who is willing to be counted as nothing, the prince of this world is powerless. The demons of pride, impatience and jealousy will not obsess such a one, for he will have abandoned all that these powers can lay hold on.

Occasionally, for a brief space, we think we have gained the victory, but the cruel obsession resumes its empire. This is because our will is weak and inconstant. Only grace can help us here; only the gifts of the Holy Spirit—of understanding and wisdom—can fortify our judgment, the supernatural rectitude of which is the decisive factor in this matter. The gift of wisdom is something we must ask of God, by persevering and humble prayer; a prayer which will be all the more likely to be heard the more it is contemplative prayer. For the justice of our judgment depends above all upon the way in which we look upon things with our mind. If the soul is habitually turned towards God, if it looks continually to him, it will come at last to learn the blessed forgetfulness of all that is not his love. There you have the sovereign means which, taking things at their source, at their highest level, creates true harmony and the perfect balance of our whole being.

May Mary, the Mother and model of all contemplatives, obtain for us from her divine Child, on this feast of his manifestation, that interior liberty and its eternal fruit.

The Nativity of Mary

⟋⟍⟋⟍

*My sister, my spouse, is a garden
enclosed, a garden enclosed, a
fountain sealed up*
> Canticle of Canticles iv, 12.

To be a contemplative is to be receptive of the
divine Word; to possess him spiritually, and to
live a life of union with him. Our Blessed Lady
is in truth the model for all contemplatives. She
is the Mother of Truth as she is of Fair Love. Our
part is to imitate her as faithful and generous
children.

The various symbols that illustrate for us the
mystery of Mary's mission—Tower of Ivory, House
of Gold, a Fountain sealed, Mirror of Justice, Ark of
the Covenant—are at the same time symbols of the
soul that loves and possesses God in an interior
solitude. Mary's virtues, the gifts she reveals and
that radiate from her, are the essential virtues, the
very conditions and special marks of the contemplative life.

According to the hymn we sing at Vespers on
all her feasts, Mary is distinguished by her
graciousness among women—among so many virgins and mothers on whom God has also bestowed
the grace of gentleness, yet whose very gentleness
is at the same time their power and strength. But
all that is both virginal and maternal Mary, the
second and spiritual Eve, possesses to an exceptional degree.

We are told that gentleness is the summing-up of all the Christian virtues: it consists, above all, of patience and kindness; of respect and love for souls, indeed for all animate being; since one who is gentle is gentle towards all living things. And this, because in its root it derives from harmony with the will of God under all its forms, a tender acquiescence in all that is. It is also the primary requisite for all who long to clarify and liberate their inward vision. There is no contemplative life without infinite patience; light only penetrates souls at rest. Tranquillity is the first disposition necessary, then, if the depths of the soul are to become translucent. The art of contemplating divine truths is the art of remaining still.

Gentleness is the quality of a forgiving and merciful soul, and is inseparable from true intellectual insight. When the mind is purified and sees all beings in their proper light, it cannot but be confident and loving. St John of the Cross has remarked with great insistence how essential kindness is for all interior progress. Our vocation is truly virginal and a mirror of Mary's. She had no need to condemn the world; it was the world that broke its strength against her graciousness. So, too, with the contemplative. Our mission is not to judge men, but to live with God.

Another of Our Lady's virtues which dazzles us, and which was pre-eminent in her, is her purity. Mary is, as it were, the very incarnation of purity, which in turn is so intimately bound up with the gift of wisdom that one can call it the indispensable virtue of the contemplative. It is not merely a question of avoiding the sins of the flesh, but of a delicacy of spirit which shields and reserves itself for the highest joys. To be pure is to know how to establish and maintain solitude of soul for God alone; to reconstruct our Garden of Eden interiorly. We know how Mary is pre-figured in the earthly Paradise, a sacred reserve inaccessible to the world; a place of delights without blemish or discord, prepared for the new Adam. Such is the contemplative soul: an en-closed garden where one has the joy of receiving directly the divine life in a stillness comparable to that which doubtless reigned at the dawn of the world. Neither thing nor person must come between the soul and God; nothing but that chaste liberty of the dawn of creation. Then a new creation takes place, and is renewed through-out time: the generation of the Son of God in us.

What conclusions can we deduce from these brief reflections on the resemblance which draws Mary's soul and ours together? We shall make the resolution to close our minds to all alien preoccupations, and by our recollection drink deeply of the innermost springs of our being. Like Mary, we shall reserve ourselves for joys not of this world, holding on to those joys through all our sufferings, all our separations, all our fears, till they attain their plenitude and enfold our whole being with their consoling peace, bringing us at last to that eternal felicity which we shall know to be the only true joy, when the shadow of this world shall have passed away.

EXALTATION OF THE HOLY CROSS

〜〜

THE Cross is the sign of the divine sacrifice, and
of the reconciliation between heaven and earth. It
is also the symbol of that union which charity
should effect between men, which Our Lord
prayed for on the eve of the Passion he willed to
undergo in order that we might be made perfect
in unity: *ut sint ipsi consummati in unum . . . that they
may be made perfect in one.*[1]

This union with others can only be realized by
means of our progress in the spiritual life, and in
the measure in which we turn away from all that is
external in order to be united with God. A man in
a state of grace is, indeed, a kind of world, at the
centre of which God never ceases to be and to act.
But this reality is only transmitted to our conscious-
ness in a partial and imperfect manner, and in a
still more incomplete and imperfect way externally
to our outward showing. Every human being is,
therefore, an enigma: a divine utterance, at once
veiled and yet manifested in the flesh by word and
deed. It is the task of patient charity to decipher
these enigmas, to discover their true meaning
beneath their uncertain and faltering expressions.
Were we but more faithful to the life of grace within
us, every soul in whom this life is present would be
pleasing to us; would be a source of peace and joy.
A life of recollection and joy of the spirit does
more than make us kindly disposed and indulgent;

[1] John xviii, 23.

it creates and preserves in our soul a true concord, which enables it to vibrate in harmony with the divine touch, wherever the latter makes itself felt. It is God himself living in us, who recognizes God within our neighbour, and welcomes him with a smile.

By conversation and activity men strive to avoid solitude; they are constantly seeking to establish contacts binding them to others. Among religious, these external relations are reduced to a minimum, though they are not entirely suppressed. A wisdom born of experience has regulated the amount of recreation in our life, and we must profit by it to avoid remaining strangers to one another; gently applying ourselves to maintain good feeling. But this requires a certain effort, for inasmuch as we reveal ourselves externally, we translate into our words and actions but a tiny part of the divine truth present within us—a poor translation it is true, which is always something of a betrayal and which, more often than not, sets us in opposition to one another rather than otherwise. Worldly folk—that is to say those who are superficial (and we are all worldly in so far as we are superficial)—find it difficult to get on well with one another. The terrible conflicts which are rending the world today are the result of a universal lack of the interior life. If we would keep the heritage of peace and joy that Our Lord bequeathed to us; if we would preserve spiritual joy in our midst, we must forget ourselves, forget one another, in order to find ourselves (and one another) again in God. For it is in him alone that creatures can meet and be truly united.

One important factor in this struggle is to know how to distinguish what is essential from what is accidental. We have said that good will and the life of grace—which are the things that matter essentially—can manifest themselves in a soul in many ways. There is a life of faith and love common to the whole Church of Christ; there are, on the other hand, enthusiasms, personal and accidental preferences, which can be legitimate and profitable for certain souls. But to want to impose them on others, and to be annoyed because others do not share them with us, is an error of judgment, the consequences of which are fatal from the point of view of charity. To put the accent or stress on the wrong note is to destroy harmony, which can only be maintained between souls who have an instinctive feeling and zeal for what is essential.

This essentially interior attitude of the soul resolutely inclined towards the sacred centre within it, calls for many sacrifices. It has to deny itself much personal and sensible satisfaction. When we enter religion we leave behind us mere human tenderness, and the continuance of this sacrifice is one of the conditions of religious friendship, as it is a condition of the interior life. But it is not only impassioned feelings that must be strenuously eschewed; it is all attachment to personal tastes, even those which seem to be spiritual, so long as they tend to cramp us in a narrow circle instead of leaving us free to surrender ourselves to that infinite liberty which God must have, and which he desires to maintain in the soul's solitude with him.

When it is a question of explaining the spirit of our vocation, or of defining how we must live it if it is to be a communion amongst ourselves in union with God, one always comes back to the practice of solitude and silence. A certain aptitude for silence, both external and internal, is essential if the soul is to be recollected and attain to mutual union in the hearts of Jesus and Mary. That wordless conversation, that friendship which springs from a detachment from all that is not God, is a very noble and precious treasure which we must jealously guard. May the Cross and the sign of the Cross be a constant invitation to us to return to the source of eternal charity, through the heart's full and unreserved assent to the sacrifice which sets it free.

The Immaculate Conception

ഇ

Come, my sister and my bride . . .
who is she that cometh as the dawn?
cf. Canticle of Canticles iv, 8 and vi, 9

In the Canticle of Canticles Our Lady is compared to the dawn, since she is the source of a
new creation. With her Immaculate Conception
the story of the human race is begun again; all is
clear once more. It is from that perfectly pure
and docile matter that the new Adam will be
fashioned. So, too, will it be with us if we allow
ourselves to be born again. For the Blessed Virgin
awaits but our good will and that whole-hearted
gesture of filial abandonment to enfold us in her
innocence. It is for us to turn unhesitatingly to
her, of whose gaze the Canticle of Canticles says:
Thy eyes are deep, like the pools at Hesebon,[1] likening it
to limpid waters in which we are cleansed and freed
from ourselves, that we may be inundated with
divine life.

Under the influence of grace, of that grace with
which Mary is full and which she dispenses in her
maternal love, the reward is proferred before the
meriting; riches and happiness poured out before
the testing time. For that is the way things are
done in this new world, a way truly divine. Men are
incapable of such liberality, since they do not
possess within them the source of good, but are
only the anxious and timid guardians of it. In all

[1] cf. Canticle of Canticles vii, 4.

our dealings with others, in the education of our children, in commerce and in the dispensation of justice, we preface our awards with conditions and the threat of punishments; the prize is given after the trial or in return for services or as a guarantee.

With God it is not so. The moment the sinner calls upon God he receives that which is beyond all price, namely the heritage of the Precious Blood and the dignity of a son. His heart is freed by the triumph of Christ, and carried away by that divine victory. And it is only then that, armed with his new dignity, he is invited to take part in the combat. Then, in his turn, he gives of himself, suffering travail and pain in the measure of his strength. Such is God's way in his kingdom, and such the wisdom of the Mother of God; such the good husbandry of the House of Gold. God's ways are different from our ways, so much so that we do not understand them. We dare not lay claim to the dignity, the liberty that is offered us; we even doubt the generosity of God himself. We heed not his gifts that are so essential to us, while we use and abuse the worthless goods of this world. And this lack of faith and confidence paralyses us; our strength fails us on the wandering path along which we struggle, for fear and anguish stifle what little good there is in us.

Open your eyes, then, and your heart, in an undisturbed solitude with God alone. Be still, and see what he is offering you, what he *is* to you. Our courage, like our patience, can only be unshakeable when it proceeds from a deep joy.

It would almost seem at times that we are afraid to recognize sanctity; as if sanctity were like material advantages, of which we are deprived if someone else takes hold of them. This shows a complete ignorance of the reality in question. What is given to the saints, what was given first to Mary, is given to us all. Such is the case with spiritual gifts, since their source is infinite and their essence charity. We retain them precisely when we renounce them—by passing them on, holding nothing back.

Take your fill, then, of the privileges that Mary offers us so abundantly. With her, our Mother and our sister, sate your hunger for God. *Venite et comedite . . . come and eat your fill.*[2]

[2] cf. Canticle of Canticles v, 1.

The Immaculate Conception (2)

೧೪೨

VIRGIN all excelling, meek among mankind... It
is thus that Mary is described in the hymn we
recite every day,[1] and it is concerning her meekness that I would meditate with you for a few
moments.

The Gospel tells us that the meek shall inherit
the earth; but it also reminds us that the kingdom
of heaven suffereth violence, and that the violent
shall bear it away.[2] The paradox disappears when
we realize that in this spiritual warfare we must be
meek towards others, but violent in the unhesi-
tating promptitude with which we answer the call
of divine Love. It is exactly the opposite of what
the unspiritual man does. He is brutal towards
others, but interiorly without any zeal for justice or
passion for truth. The violence of the spiritual man
is inseparable from his meekness, which is quickly
lost if he does not know how to meet with a categ-
orical refusal the lie which hides itself in all excuses
or softness towards oneself. To dismiss all interior
discussion with a Yes or No, that resoluteness which
Our Lord recommends to us, is the very first condition that must be fulfilled if the soul is to
disentangle itself and be given the marvellous grace
of meekness.

This virtue which distinguished our Blessed Lady
among all women, cannot but be a most necessary

[1] *Virgo singularis, inter omnes mitis*... from the hymn *Ave
maris stella*, at Vespers of Our Lady.
[2] Matthew v, 4 and xi, 12.

virtue. Note first that Mary's meekness is, as it were, a reflection of God's. Mary is, indeed, a pure mirror, so free from all shadow of self, that the divine Essence finds its perfection fully reflected in her humility. That is why the Immaculate Virgin can be an object of contemplation, since her purity so mirrors that of God that we see him, who is Pure Act, in her.

For meekness is a disposition truly divine. Violence proceeds from an authority conscious of its weakness. God has no need to break us in order to impose his will; his meekness is only another name for his all-powerfulness. Mary, on the other hand, is all-obedient, and it is in her total abandonment that she comes very close to God's omnipotence. To abandon all pretensions to self-love without a struggle; to consent quietly to all that is asked of us: it is this that makes us resemble Mary, and allows us to partake of her graciousness and power. For God refuses us nothing—he can refuse nothing—provided we abandon ourselves to him with all our heart.

Meekness towards creatures is the result of patience and of respect for them. It has been said of meekness that it is the crown of the Christian virtues: indeed almost more than a virtue. It is, indeed, a unique grace, which penetrates one's whole being, and influences one's whole conduct; it even extends its influence to beings lower than man, to things inanimate. A meek person does even the simplest things in a different way from those who are not meek. Wisdom is meek; so too is understanding, since one must necessarily respect an object if one is to understand it. What is more, meekness implies sympathy; it wrests their secret from beings who would withdraw into themselves in face of impulsiveness as they would from violence. Meekness is both virginal and maternal; without it the approach to souls can never be deep or effective.

We have said that meekness is the fruit of patience and of respect. Of patience above all. A soul will not be meek unless it is firmly resolved repeatedly to forgo its rights, and to suffer continuously, at times cruelly. On the other hand, it is true that meekness disarms our adversaries, and robs suffering of its venom. Our suffering, for the most part, comes from revolt, from a want of adaptability and abandonment.

It is true that we must do violence to ourselves if we would cease to be violent; but in a manner more general and profound, the respect and patience which, in imitation of Mary and even of God himself, we must acquire in our relations with others, we have need of also towards ourselves. We need much patience with our own soul, to say nothing of the body. All the natural energy in the world (so Our Lord said[3]) will not enable us to change to any appreciable degree the character, unsatisfactory as it is in general, which our nature and upbringing have provided for us. But anyone who recognizes himself frankly for what he is; who by that fact alone is freed from the temptation to criticize others, and who in spite of

[3] cf. Matthew vi, 27.

71

his self-knowledge does not omit to renew his effort every day, keeping his eyes fixed on God, persevering for God's sake alone and counting solely on his bounty—such a one, I say, does more than grow better; he leaves and abandons himself to God, to whom such loving humility gives more glory than all success. Each one of us must respect his soul, remembering that it comes from God and belongs lovingly to him; welcoming the action of the Holy Spirit in it, whatever form that action may take. The soul is so delicate that only God can handle it.

Let us, then, beg of our Blessed Lady something of her meekness. It is she who shields us for God, and makes us chaste in the highest sense: that is to say, free from all resistance, awaiting the coming of our Spouse.

> *Virgo singularis,*
> *Inter omnes mitis,*
> *Nos culpis solutos*
> *Mites fac et castos.*[4]

[4] Virgin all excelling,
Meek among mankind,
Win for us our pardon,
Make us chaste and kind.

SUNDAY WITHIN THE OCTAVE OF THE PURIFICATION

∽∽

O N the actual day of the feast of the Purification, you were encouraged to meditate on this mystery, but it seems we might do so again. Then, it was of Mary's humility that we spoke; but one can see also in the Purification the feast of light, with the connection the Church wishes to establish between the words of Simeon and the blessing of the fire. Today, however, we would recall a more profound mystery, seeing in the Purification the feast of the priesthood of Mary.

Let us first consider what we learn from Scripture of the actions of Mary on this day. She comes up to the Temple, a very young mother, of perhaps sixteen years, swathed in her veils beneath which she hides the Child Jesus. St Joseph, her spouse and guardian, accompanies her, carrying the two turtle doves in a cage, and the five silver pieces in a purse. Would that we could imitate her recollection and guess her thoughts at that moment. At the porch of the Temple she presents one turtle dove to the priest, and is sprinkled with the water of purification. Next, she mounts the steps to offer the five pieces of silver and the second dove. Then she enters the Temple, and at last is in the presence of the Father, towards whom she holds out her Child—the Son of God, and her son. And she knows that all humanity is contained within this tiny being. All the efforts, all the sufferings, all the joys of Christians are even then in the heart of

Jesus, and Mary offers to the Father all the children who will be hers. Doubtless this thought is present to her mind; she knows that this act of hers has an infinite value and significance. Already, at that moment, she was loving us in her virginal heart, and was offering us to the Father. In truth, all our life ought to consist in preparing ourselves to be offered by Mary. All our actions, all our thoughts, should be such that she can offer them to God.

That we may arrive at this sublime offering, the first condition, then, is to lead a pure and upright life. For us (as religious) rectitude lies obviously in the path traced out by our Rule. It is a tremendous advantage to lead a life so utterly simple as ours, where the difficulties, the intrigues and the ambitions that disturb the hearts of people in the world have no place. Our life is like the unleavened bread, all pure and white, that the priest is about to consecrate. A religious who does his simple duty is quite ready for this offering and consecration.

The second condition is solitude of heart. Our heart is a temple greater than that at Jerusalem. We must be alone in this temple, with God and Our Lady. Far from disturbing our solitude with God, Mary assures it. There must be a great silence there, too, and a great calm; no noise, above all no contention. Should we be discontented with our superiors or with our fellow brethren; if we pass judgment on them; or if we are occupied interiorly with complaining, making comparisons of situations and people, then the temple of our heart is not still, and the offering of all we do cannot have its full effect. Neither must there be any curiosity or impatience. Not only must our heart be free from solicitude in all that concerns others, but it must also be free from all anxiety in regard to ourselves. Needless to say, we must be sorry for our sins and, above all, do all we can to grow better every day; but the thought of our imperfections must never become a preoccupation. It is God we must think of, not ourselves. To be glad because we are in a certain place, and upset because we are not somewhere else—so long as such thoughts occupy our minds, Mary cannot exercise in us her virginal priesthood.

Solitude of heart, as thus understood, comes very near to spiritual abandonment, which is the third condition necessary for a soul that is to become an offering pleasing to God at the hands of Mary. We must hand over to her all our cares, place ourselves in her hands for everything; attain, in a word, the carefree spirit of a child. All the advice of spiritual writers on this point is nothing compared to the strong words of the Gospel. *Be not solicitous for tomorrow*, says Our Lord; *be not solicitous for your life, what you shall eat, nor for your body what you shall put on.*[1] We are to be like the birds and flowers of the field, which are committed to the sole care of their heavenly Father: yet does he not bring them to perfection?[2] We are not to look back at what has

[1] Matthew vi, 34 and 25.
[2] cf. Matthew vi, 26, 28 ff.

passed; not even give these things so much as a thought; our right hand is to be in ignorance of what our left hand does.[3] Finally, St Peter sums it all up in one command: *Cast all your care upon him, for he hath care of you.*[4] The verb which he uses here suggests the action of throwing overboard all that encumbers a vessel threatened with shipwreck. Let us, then, shut our eyes and place ourselves in Our Lady's hands, and allow her to take charge of us and offer us to God.

It is the same whether we are happy and enjoying spiritual delights, or cast down and depressed. We must close our eyes and act exactly as though we knew nothing about our state—abandon ourselves, in other words. Never mind whether you are thought well of—that should not worry anyone who has deliberately closed his eyes to these things. The same applies to our judgments of the faults or virtues of others: leave all that to Mary. Oh, my dear Brothers, I can assure you that if you will abandon yourselves thus, Our Lady will not fail to take you in her arms and offer you to the Father. The whole secret of going from this world to God is to shut one's eyes and leave the guiding to Our Lady.

On the other hand, do not think that such abandonment is opposed to generosity. Those who sincerely practise abandonment will always be docile to the inspirations of grace. They possess what the Abbé de St Cyran called *flexibility* in the

[3] cf. Luke ix, 62 and Matthew vi, 3.
[4] 1 Peter v, 7.

hands of God. It is a gift of childhood: a child, as you know, allows himself to be led by his mother. So the three conditions that we have enumerated for this offering of ourselves at the hands of Mary—recollection, abandonment and generosity—always go together, and are in fact inseparable.

See, then, what we shall be if we are to prepare ourselves to be offered in the Temple by Mary—faithful, tranquil, simple and trustful; blind as one becomes blind through an excess of light. Then will she carry us in her arms, and each of our actions, offered by her to the Father, will have an infinite value. For a soul thus abandoned there are no longer any little things. To fulfil the most ordinary household duties—everything is so precious when offered at Mary's hands. In the same way, we may say without contradiction that for such souls there are also no longer any big things. What appears to be a mountain and a formidable obstacle to anyone who tries to be his own guide and makes himself responsible for his own care, is a thing of no account to an 'abandoned' soul. I am not esteemed; others think poorly of me and deem me good for nothing . . . I am terribly upset by such thoughts, so long as I have the responsibility of myself. How am I to justify myself? A renewed zeal for justice and truth (or the contrary) works me up into a miserable state of ferment at the mere thought of such a thing . . . Mary's child hardly notices it! It is no concern of his: he keeps his eyes shut, holds fast his Mother's hands, and allows himself to be led whithersoever she pleases.

As before, she quickly lifts us up in her arms, and we no longer see what seems so terrible to others.

We are in truth caught between two fires. You are probably aware of that expression, taken from military language, which indicates the position of an army attacked simultaneously from the rear and in front. For us it is the fire of love that besieges us on all sides. In front of us is the Father's face, the Blessed Trinity waiting for us; behind, the virginal love of Mary, offering us to God. The spiritual life consists precisely in allowing ourselves to be led, lifted up and borne by those maternal hands, so that we may be presented to the eternal Father.

It is a lovely thing, indeed, to feel oneself abandoned into those pure hands. How sure one is of not straying; what assurance does not their very purity impart? And those hands have the power, also, to purify us. We have already suggested this interpretation of the feast of which we are celebrating the octave: it is the feast of the purification of humanity. Mary had no need of purification; but we need it, everyone of us, if we are to receive Jesus, the Light of the Father. It is only pure crystal, indeed, which allows light to pass through it. Thus Mary went to the Temple, not for her own sake but for ours: in our name, in order to share her virginal purity with us, so that we might in turn receive Jesus. That is why the Immaculate Virgin knelt humbly at the porch of the Temple. And the priest who sprinkled her with the water of purification must surely have wondered at that Mother, little more than a child, whose countenance was clearer and purer than the dawn. Surely he must have paused, hesitating; guessing, perhaps, that this water was not for her, but would overflow on to the whole of humanity, prostrate in the shadows, thirsting for pardon. . . .

So it is that Mary wishes to communicate something of her grace to us; to let the waves from her immaculate heart overflow to us.

And, finally, she lifts us up in her arms and presents us to the Father. He gazes unceasingly at us, and we at him. This 'face to face' is the highest form of the interior life: it is thus that St Paul describes heaven. We shall no longer see him, he says, in the mirror of creatures, but 'face to face'.[5]

When we live under his glance, all that we do is lit up; everything becomes clearer and more translucent. As soon as an evil thought comes to us—of anger, for example, or of spite or revenge—a shadow is cast, and we withdraw from God's gaze. How often Holy Scripture uses the expression: *ambulavit coram Deo . . . he walked with God,*[6] to make us realize the brightness and beauty of a life truly consecrated to God.

But we, too, we look at him . . . and it is his countenance we see, the Face of Love, and we are no longer afraid. No more need we turn away our gaze, as we must needs do, did not Our Blessed Lady liberate us from all fear and strengthen us in our trust. We look at God: his gaze and that of the soul meet, and merge in an eternal union.

[5] 1 Corinthians xiii, 12.   [6] cf. Genesis v, 24 and vi, 9.

79

∽∽

THE Holy Spirit, from whom we can and should receive an out-pouring on this feast, if we will only open our hearts to him, is the Spirit of childhood. It is he who enables us to recognize ourselves as sons of God, giving us, as St Paul says, love and confidence in our Father in heaven. It is this characteristic of children of God that distinguishes us from those who do not believe; indeed, it is this that makes us Christians. If we would define exactly what the attitude of a son implies, we will see that it comes from three things: submission, liberty and joy. I place submission first, because, indeed, it is quite impossible to be a true child of God if one has not, to begin with, the generosity of obedience. We, in particular, must know how to turn our backs on our own tastes and ideas, and allow ourselves to be moulded by our Rule, and by all that community life involves. And we must set about this manfully, neither reasoning nor looking back. Only one who has made a sacrifice of this kind, even if it is only once, knows what wonderful independence and interior freedom it gives to the soul.

For spiritual childhood also comprises liberty: a liberty which is the daughter of submission, of a simple and generous abandonment. *Ubi spiritus, ibi libertas* ... says St Paul: *where the spirit of the Lord is, there is liberty;*[1] a liberty, of its nature

---

[1] Corinthians iii, 17.

interior, which consists in not being attached to one's self-love. Such a liberty is only to be attained by devotedness and recollection. Your work and your prayers tend constantly to make you free, and you will attain to this independence all the sooner in so far as you are faithful to the one and to the other. The Holy Spirit, moreover, is a Spirit of joy; for how can one fail to be happy if one is freed from one's chains? Man's great sorrow is that he feels himself a prisoner to his own selfishness; he is his own warder and alone knows how difficult it is to liberate himself. But each act of obedience, of charity and humility emancipates the heart, which leaps upwards (so it would seem), just as a bird takes flight the moment its cage is opened.

You are not unfamiliar with this joy, of which you have each received a gracious portion. And you would like to communicate it to others; to those dear to you, to the loved ones you left behind when you came here; to all the poor folk who suffer, so often without knowing why.

Well, the only way to radiate this consolation to other hearts is to make your own heart a furnace of confidence and love, in short to allow the Heart of Jesus to live in you.

In a family or community it is already something if we can show to others a calm and serene exterior; a sad face casts a shadow around it. But great as is such an influence, it is nothing compared to that of a soul in which divine Love dwells. Men today have invented and fashioned for themselves enormous power-houses of energy, which spread waves all over the world. When our spirit is radiant with divine light and love, full of the Spirit of God, is it surprising that it, too, should shed its rays far and wide?

Among all men there is a certain solidarity. We depend upon others who, along with us, struggle and suffer. Brothers and Fathers, religious and lay-folk alike, we are all collaborators: together we are building the City of God. In one way, this is a charge on us, since we know that others are looking to us for help; but it is a support for us also, since what we give we receive back a hundredfold. The only way to receive grace in abundance is to give all that one has.

Let us, then, ask the Holy Spirit to give us that patience, that promptitude, to give gladly whatever is asked of us; that supernatural gaiety, in short, which is the sign of his presence, and the condition of his reign in us. And may he make us sources of life for others, as he did of Mary, his spouse, full of grace.

ALL SAINTS

∽∽

MANY who try our life complain after a very short
time that the monastic life is too easy, that life in
a Charterhouse does not come up to their expec-
tations in the matter of heroic austerity.
Nevertheless it is very often these same people who
have expressed disappointment, who give up after
a little while, for the very opposite reason—they
now find it more than they bargained for! We must
not be surprised at this apparent contradiction;
nor is it confined to novices. The fact is that the
spiritual life, being a spiritual childhood, is at once
too humble for our pride and too exacting for the
sensual man.

Our Lord tells us in the Gospels that the way of
salvation is hard. The gate by which we must enter
is, he reminds us, a narrow one.[1] Yet he assures us
that his yoke is easy and his burden light.[2] It is
good to meditate on both these truths, and see in
what way they do not contradict one another.

As a matter of fact, anyone who wants to love
distrusts whatever is easy. Such souls abhor the
easy way. They know by experience from their
own shortcomings how easy it is to slip down
from what is facile to the mediocre and vulgar.
This is true on the natural plane. As men, we
are under a necessity to wage a continuous war
on ourselves if we are not to deteriorate and sink
lower than nature. We are pledged to an interior

---

[1] Matthew vii, 14.   [2] Matthew xi, 30.

struggle, and we must accept it and hold on to it patiently. This constant effort is a burden; so, too, does the spiritual life involve struggle and effort. Anyone who fails to realize this is hopelessly blind.

But whilst it is necessary to be on our guard against any kind of softness, on the other hand it is not true that the spiritual life means always looking for trouble. To make it our aim to undertake certain things which cannot fail to excite the admiration of others (or our own!) is to miss completely the whole point of the spiritual life. It is true that the life of the spirit cannot bear any kind of *laissez-faire*, but at the same time it is not a form of athletics. It lives by charity. Now nothing is so simple as love; hence there is one kind of difficulty that a soul in love with God will avoid at all costs, and that is complexity in any form whatsoever. What is true is *simple*, what is false is complex. Simplicity is God's sign-manual.

Whenever I look within myself I am lost in the complications of self-love, and the suffering caused thereby is fruitless. If I spend myself on others, they only lead me back to myself by the vicious circle of my passions. The soul that waits on God, patiently and unhurriedly, receives on the contrary the simple assurance that it is infinitely loved; and with that answer comes a call to love with all one's strength here and now, an answer which resolves all our problems. This is the most effective and fundamental way to simplify our lives; to become true contemplatives, with no other desire but to remain alone with

God in solitude. There is another way, which is inseparable from what I have just mentioned, and that is a frank generosity. If a soul, especially in the case of a religious, dreams of stopping half-way, it is in vain that it will endeavour to keep going, and it will only waste its strength if it tries to do so. Only the best suffices if we are to keep an even keel. The right we reserve to ourselves to retain our self-love up to a certain point, as we say, acts like poison in the soul. On the contrary, to risk all releases the soul, whilst to give all raises it to breathe freely the air of the heights. There is nothing *simpler* than pure faith and complete abandonment.

This attitude, interior and absolute, has practical consequences in other directions. If we are simple with God, we shall be simple with men. Any want of simplicity with our superiors or with our spiritual guide arises from a mixture of vanity and distrust, and is opposed to a childlike spirit. The quiet of contemplation should cure us of this fear and pride.

We are wanting in that simplicity with our brethren when we become super-sensitive and sus- picious. Here again the pretence of being someone, the want of concentration on the essen- tials, makes us see difficulties where God has not put them. If only we can keep ourselves more and more under the rays of the divine presence, we shall forget ourselves and become serene and pure of heart. Only the beauty of God contemplated in its essence, or in Love crucified or as seen in the immaculate countenance of Mary, can deliver us from ourselves: it alone can captivate us. And this is what Our Lord meant when he said: *The truth shall make you free.*[3]

In conclusion, I would say just this. The way of love, above all the way of the contemplative, is not an easy one. It calls for the total gift of self. But neither is it strictly speaking difficult, since it has marvellous advantages and the divine prerogative of simplicity.

May Our Lady and the saints whose feast we keep today obtain for us this interior liberty, and may love faithfully preserved bring us to that vision, in the union of the soul with God, which will be our eternal joy.

[3] John viii, 32.

صصص

WHENEVER God wants to bring about the beginning of a new life, he prepares a sacred place, a haven of purity and silence, where his action can be welcomed unreservedly, safe from all interruption. All beginnings are thus undertaken in recollection and silence. We see this at Bethlehem. Jesus came to be born, not amidst the clamour of a city nor in a crowded public place, but in a mysterious cave, a sacred retreat carved in a rock. And hidden therein—a virgin: the most chaste, the most silent, and the most humble of creatures. And it was in the heart of that Virgin, where no earthly desire penetrated, that God elected to give himself to mankind.

Well, it is such analogous conditions as these that each of us must realize if we are to receive the life of grace, and assure our growth until Christ himself lives in us. A Charterhouse is a place where Our Lord wants to be born anew: it is a replica of the cave at Bethlehem, and is a mirror of Mary herself. It is a haven of solitude and silence, where our soul is set apart for God alone, and by the very fact invites him to fulfil his highest work, which is to communicate his joy.

But a Charterhouse will not be that Virgin and Mother of the life of grace in us, unless we are faithful to its (and her) spirit. By recollection and detachment, we must do all we can to keep our purity of soul.

One of the first faults we are liable to commit

against solitude is to remain attached to the world and to our family. No one would wish us to do anything but retain all our love for our parents and those dear to us: indeed, we ought to love them always with an even purer love. If they are in need or are suffering, we should suffer too. But we must learn to leave them to God. And if we suffer, we should do so with confidence and perfect abandonment, so much so that suffering unites us to God still more, instead of being a distraction turning us away from our vocation.

Another fault against solitude, which has even the appearance of a good intention, is to worry ourselves about others, for whom we are not responsible. We should—and must—aid those with whom we live, but *spiritually*; and we do so by being devoted to them and ready to serve them, but avoiding all gossip and scandal, and above all always remaining ourselves united to Our Lord. Then the gentle flame of charity will shed its light around us, and will contribute to maintain in our religious home that atmosphere of peace, which is a preparation for heaven, while consoling and sanctifying ourselves. Unfortunately, there is an interior talkativeness, which lies at the root of the exterior, and does us much harm. Instead of thinking of the reality of the divine Love who invites us to serve him in the present moment, we indulge in day-dreams, we think of the past, of the future, of what we could do in the world, in circumstances that are purely imaginary.

Or we encourage over and over again thoughts

that are critical of others, or that concern the management of the house. Or, again, we brood over our troubles. I know that interior silence is not easy, and it will always be imperfect. At the same time, we must apply ourselves to it with great patience. Our heart is so indiscreet: it is that which betrays us. If we could keep our heart still, the devil would be baffled, and temptations would find nothing in us to take hold of.

The object of our efforts to preserve our solitude and the spirit of recollection is not merely to assure our calm and preserve our balance; it is a question of co-operating with a supreme desire of God which he wants to realize in our soul, by giving birth therein to his Son. Be the life of a religious as humble and hidden as you will, the love which reigns in his soul is something for the whole of humanity. For the world has need of love, for love alone gives joy. And grace is of itself fruitful; it cannot burn within us without lighting up other souls.

May the Blessed Virgin, hidden and silent in the cave of Bethlehem, help us to imitate her in her recollectedness and purity; in her fidelity as spouse of the Holy Spirit, and in her generosity as the Mother of souls.

THE FLOWER OF THE FIELD

つぃの

I am the flower of the field,
and the lily of the valleys . . .
Canticle of Canticles ii, 1.

THESE words from the Canticle of Canticles are
generally applied by theologians to Our Lady,
whom the Litany of Loretto also calls the *Mystical
Rose.* In choosing these words, our first wish is to
place under Mary's patronage such considerations
as we hope to submit to you on the subject of
spiritual simplicity and abandonment of the soul
to divine Providence. These are the very virtues that
we find exemplified in that chapter of St Matthew,
where Our Lord uses the words: *Consider the lilies
of the field;*[1] and who, indeed, more than Our Lady
has given us such a perfect example of them?
Before anything else, therefore, I would ask her to
obtain for you all the graces of which she has so
worthily merited to be the dispensatrix, through
her virginal purity and her perfect abandonment
to the divine Will.

Simplicity is the sister of purity and not less of
poverty; since it is the treasure from which we draw
the very means for these virtues. A simple soul does
not waste time on half-measures; it goes straight to
the end in everything, and with one movement—
one bound, as it were—arrives at the very heart of
God.

But this does not mean that we are to despise

[1] Matthew vi, 28.

the gifts of grace, nor for that matter any of the aids we need so badly during our earthly pilgrimage. For these signs come from God himself, and are the means by which we shall find him and serve him in this life. More than that, he has given us his Son, whom he called the Way and the Mediator; for it is through him, indeed, that salvation comes to us, and by him alone that we shall reach our goal.

The fulness of Christ, in whom as St Paul says are united all things, draws souls to him by countless different ways. The ineffable richness of divine Being cannot but manifest itself under divers aspects. Apart from the natural plane, we can extend our legitimate devotions to the various aspects of Our Lord's Person: to Our Lady's part in mirroring the light of Christ and drawing us to him; and equally to the sacramental and liturgical aids that the Church spreads before us so lavishly. These ways or manifestations of divine Providence are numberless and varied, by reason of the very simplicity of divine grace, and of our imperfect capacity for receiving it.

These powerful and effective signs, however, exist for our sakes, as means. They invite us to seek farther with eager zeal the very centre towards which they beckon us. Thus devotion to the Incarnate Word leads us to worship him in spirit; his sacred humanity to his divinity. It is precisely for the contemplation of this latter that the whole work of redemption and grace is directed.

Our senses content themselves with appearances, for they are external faculties made for the mere surface of things. But our intellect (as the word indicates) seeks to penetrate whatever object is put before it, that it may reach the reality behind these appearances. The German mystics, however, seem to find beyond the intellect a faculty reserved for God alone, and dominatingly impatient of all intermediary means. Reason—so they tell us—makes use of concepts and words, but what makes a man spiritual is the craving for *contact.* Hungry for solitude, hungry for God alone, this faculty forces its very way beyond all bounds and measures, beyond names and images, that it may find the Essence Itself, and rest quietly therein alone.

It would be foolish and unwise to pretend to the higher forms of the spiritual life and neglect the ordinary ascetical means necessary for each step of the way, or not make wise and prudent use of the resources placed at our disposal by the Church for the help and sanctification of the faithful. But no school of spiritual thought can be reproached for aiming too high, since our inward vision is made for pure light, and the soul only truly breathes on the heights. In everything it is true wisdom to seek the source. So true is this as a general principle that it can be applied to everything. Drink at the source of the fountain if you would taste in all their purity the gifts of both earth and heaven. If this be true of the water we drink with our lips; if it be true in the realms of art and science, it is even more so in the domain of grace. Seek the source of life within you; waste no time in getting there, and then take full measure of joy in its limpid purity.

You remember Our Lord's promise: *He that believeth in me, as the Scripture saith: out of his belly shall flow rivers of living water.*[2] It is only by slaking our thirst at the heart of Jesus that we can give to others what their souls need, and thus practise true charity towards them. Daily charity, especially among religious, consists for the most part in the giving of invisible things—the fruits of our prayers; silent and unexpressed sympathy, an understanding of and respect for those with whom we live. In order to understand the life of a religious it is of the utmost importance that we ourselves should not be victims of any sort of narrowness, but have on the contrary a lofty and simple spirituality. So long as we keep close to Our Lord, if we love him in spirit and in truth, we shall recognize and welcome all forms that that love may take. The intellect, guided by charity, seeks ever the centre and the height: our inward vision loves the summits, with their large and comprehensive view. It is there that one understands; there that one loves.

Go then, straight to the heart of Jesus: to that innermost mystery that that heart reveals; learning from God himself all powerful how to love our brethren with a pure respect for the being that God has given them, and for the many graces with which he has adorned them through his own sovereign liberty.

[2] John vii, 38.

Now supernatural generosity is a form of justice. The soul is comparable to a balance, exact and at the same time free, since it rests on a single point, and is poised in the hand of God. All freedom comes from peace in the depths of the soul. All goodness to be effective is the present and spontaneous outcome of a contemplative grace. No true consolation can be given by one soul to another unless it proceeds from a soul serene, and at rest in the peace of God.

That peace, however, is not to be found without much labour and suffering. No soul is set free until it has had the courage to break with its attachments. God takes possession of a soul in the measure in which it is freed—by patient and honest efforts—from created things. But in this daily task of ascetical detachment, we are not alone; at our hand are divine aids—the very course of events as ordered by creative Wisdom. Everything that claims our attachment is, when all is said and done, passing and doomed to die. The chains with which we bind ourselves are very fragile, and once our will is set in order by our clinging to the divine Will, everything conspires to set us free.

No doubt it will be necessary at times to take the initiative of personal effort, but the first task, especially in the religious life, is to make use of those very things that constrain us—that hem us in: the very trials and constraints which God permits to encumber our path. Keep silent: smile quietly when a treasured trifle is taken from you and causes you pain. When things go of themselves, let them go— they leave you God. They live only to die; they are given only to be taken away again, that we may be left free. A religious who welcomes ungrudgingly the mortifications that each day brings is already travelling fast on the way of interior peace, and thus of union with God. It is in this sense that the abandonment recommended by the Gospel is so true. The flower of the field labours not, neither does it spin:[3] yet the whole of nature conspires together to fulfil the designs of God in its regard. Still more does that same nature seek to bring to perfection God's designs on us. Man, alas! has the power to thwart that growth—not so, the rose. What makes the soul elect of God is its unconditional surrender to the work of divine grace: what sanctifies it is its immediate *Amen,* and the purity and reality of its consent.

Rest assured there never will be a day which will not bring its contradictions, its suffering, its salutary check. Try to find in these things the will of the Father, recognizing gratefully in them their liberating action. With a heart set freer every day, united to God in a manner closer and more intimate and interior, learn to love your neighbour by the same act by which you love God.

You have the example of Mary . . . it is her abundant blessing that I wish you in conclusion.

[3] cf. Matthew vi, 28.

THE BLESSED TRINITY
AND THE
SUPERNATURAL LIFE

PROLOGUE

ᨏᨏ

Per ipsum et cum ipso et in ipso
est tibi Deo Patri omnipotenti:
in unitate Spiritus Sancti, omnis
honor et gloria
Canon Missae

IN the pages which follow, the writer has made
no attempt to present a complete treatise on the
dogma of the most Blessed Trinity. Nor is it his
desire to treat of any particular problem of the
interior life, or to suggest new solutions. His
aim has simply been to invite the reader's atten-
tion to the more general vistas of the supernatural life. We shall view the whole horizon of
the Faith, with its practical consequences. We
shall start with the consideration of the Source—
the Blessed Trinity, the most intimate life of
God—in order to come back finally to the consummation of all things in this same mystery. The life
of all created things, and in particular the higher
and interior life of man, will thus appear as having
both its root and its end in the depths of the divine
being.

If one is to arrive at the term, it is essential that
one should know the direction. God invites us to
set out upon the way which will lead us to himself. This way we must know if we are to walk

with surety. The vision of the end will give us the desire, which will give birth to confidence, and this confidence in turn is the source of all strength.

Our humble attempt will have achieved its aim if it has helped to make us aware of our dignity as children of God. It is true that God, according to the inspired Word, dwells in light inaccessible.[1] But it is also true that thanks to the redeeming Blood of Christ we are raised to a supernatural state and are become children of God. Does not, indeed, the Apostle say: *In ipso vivimus et movemur et sumus—in him we live and move and have our being.*[2] *Filii et haeredes—sons and heirs.*[3]

It suffices—and it is, in fact, necessary—that we should live solely under the influence of the Holy Spirit if we are to become fully his 'sons'. *Qui Spiritu Dei aguntur ii sunt filii Dei—for whosoever are led by the Spirit of God, they are the sons of God.*[4] And it is by the same Spirit that the Father will become our Father: *Abba, Pater.* But there is a conflict between the Spirit of God and our narrow self-interest. Nothing will give us so great an impulse to die to ourselves as this knowledge of our true destiny. To convince ourselves of our greatness will be the surest way to make ourselves so 'little' that we keep back nothing for ourselves. Then only will we draw deep breaths of the divine life, a foretaste of our eternal happiness.

[1] 1 Timothy vi, 16.   [2] cf. Acts xvii, 28.
[3] Romans viii, 17.   [4] Romans viii, 14.

IN GOD

1. THE DOGMA

꿍ꚩ

GOD is subsistent Being itself. The word 'being'
applies strictly only to God. *Deus solus vere essentiae
nomen tenet—God alone has the name of true being.*[1]
For all other things, ourselves included, compared
to that pure and perfect substance, are not even
shadows. That is why God gave his name when
speaking to Moses as *He who is.*[2] *Tam verum enim
esse Deus habet, quod nostrum esse, suo comparatum,
nihil est—so truly has God being, that our being, compared to his, is nothing.*[3]

God is one. He possesses unity in a super-
eminent manner: or, more accurately, he is unity
itself, absolute simplicity. In him there is no distinction of parts, no accident, no change. *Hear, O
Israel, the Lord our God is one Lord.*[4] None the
less, this one God is three Persons. God is Father:
he begets a Son in a unity of nature, without division or change. And from the Father and the Son
proceeds equally the Holy Spirit. The Father is
God, the Son is God, the Holy Spirit is God;
and these three are but one and the same God.
This trinity of Persons is no less necessary than the
unity of being.

---

[1] St Jerome.   [2] Exodus iii, 14.
[3] St Bonaventure.   [4] Deuteronomy vi, 4.

The Trinity is essential to God just as much as his divine nature. The divine processions are not something added to his essence, already formed and complete: they are the very substance, the very perfection of God. To be in three Persons, Father, Son and Holy Spirit, is in reality the same as being God, although our intellect cannot grasp the equivalence of these statements. Both propositions, nevertheless, bear witness to the same necessity, and if we are able to state them separately it is because we only know God in indirect ways, in the obscurity of faith. We must be on our guard lest we attempt to measure the mystery of the Trinity by the narrowness of our weak and discursive concepts.

The divine eternity is a changeless present, wherein the Father begets the Son, and both breathe forth the Holy Spirit. St Augustine compares the Son to air, ever filled with light, receiving at every moment a renewal without change of the whole light of the sun. The divine generation did not take place at the beginning of time, once and for all. It is a divine act, or rather it is *the* divine act, eternal and unending, which never ceases and is never interrupted, any more than is the divine Being from whom, in reality, it cannot be distinguished. *Now*—at every moment of time—this act is being accomplished: the Son is born of the Father. *Ego hodie genui te—this day have I begotten thee.*[5]

The divine Persons are subsistent relations. Amongst creatures, relations such as paternity or

[5] Psalm ii, 7.

sonship are only accidents. Take away the 'accident', and the father and the son remain just men. In God, however, everything is simple, all is subsistent, all is God. That is why in the Blessed Trinity the fatherhood is the whole being of the Father, which is identical with the divine being. So, too, the sonship of the Son is the whole being of the Son, and the same holds of the Holy Spirit. According to his whole being, the Father is *ad Filium*; and, according to his whole being, the Son is *ad Patrem*. Were our supernatural vision sufficiently pure, sufficiently deep, we would see in this not only the perfect solution of the apparent contradiction between these truths—God one, yet three—but the necessity of the one included in that of the other. 'Each of the Persons' says St Gregory Nazienzen, 'refers not less to the others than to himself; and that is the reason for their reduction to unity, which is utterly beyond our comprehension.'

The divine Persons are really distinct. That is why there can exist between them those interchanges of knowledge and love, which can only belong to subsistent personalities. The Father is not the Son, nor is the Son the Father: the duality is so real and so true that it suffices to constitute the requisite number under the Old Law for the value of a witness. *If I judge, my judgment is true, because I am not alone, but I and the Father that sent me. And in your law it is written that the testimony of two witnesses is true.*[6]

Yet, although the Son is a different Person from

[6] cf. John viii, 16–17.

the Father, he is not something different: *alius non aliud.* In order to be truly the Son, he must stand in opposition to the Father by a real relation, and it is precisely this relation which brings him back into a unity of nature with the Father, a unity more perfect than any unity men can conceive.

2. THE ANALOGIES OF KNOWLEDGE AND LOVE

ଉଚ୍ଚ

In the account given in the book of Genesis, on the sixth day, before the creation of man, God spoke thus: *Let us make man to our image and likeness.*[1] The plural seems to underline the action of the three Persons. Images of God, we carry within us a certain reflection of the divine generation. The Fathers and Doctors of the Church have studied this signature of the creative Spirit engraved in our very nature, and the deductions they draw from it give us some idea of the nature of the processions which constitute the mystery of the Blessed Trinity. It is quite true that we can only approach such an understanding by a very distant analogy. Nevertheless, it is not without a providential disposition that such comparisons have been stressed by Christian thinkers who were at the same time contemplatives and saints. Their origin, their antiquity, their admirable correspondence with the scriptural texts confer on these speculations a singular authority.

A spiritual being has two vital operations—to know and to love. Now since God is being in its absolute plenitude, these two operations belong to him by necessity of essence and nature. The first vital operation of God is the act of knowing. By that act, which is his essence itself, God produces a perfect concept of what he knows perfectly; that is to say, himself. It is the procession

---

[1] Genesis i, 26.

of the interior Word. In that divine Word, God, so to speak, defines himself. The Word, that is, is the adequate expression of the Father. The Word *Logos*, which St John uses in the first chapter of his Gospel, means both *word* and *reason*; for it is the reason of God, as it is the reason of everything else. That Word is rightly called the Immaculate Mirror, the Image of the invisible God, the Splendour of his glory, and the Figure of his substance.[2]

This intelligible fruit of the divine knowledge is also called 'generated knowledge'—*notitia genita, Deus intellectus.* In so far as this essential representation of himself proceeds from him—perfectly equal and similar to its source in the unity of the same nature—God is in the truest sense called *Father.* Fatherhood belongs to God before it can ever be attributed to men. It is from that divine and primal paternity that all paternity in heaven and earth has its origin and name ... *of whom all paternity in heaven and earth is named.*[3]

The Word is thus truly the Son of God, consubstantial with the Father, co-eternal, enjoying the same omnipotence and the same immensity. Of all the ways in which a being can produce another being, the most perfect is by generation. For he who generates imparts his own nature to the one generated, and pours into that being his own life. And since no dignity can be wanting in God, generation must be found in the Godhead.

---

[2] Wisdom vii, 26; Colossians i, 5; Hebrews i, 3.
[3] Ephesians iii, 15.

*Shall not I that make others to bring forth chil-
dren, myself bring forth, saith the Lord.*[4] There
is no doubt that generation is infinitely greater
than creation, for the Creator does not give himself, whilst the Father is in the Son with his whole
being and essence. *The Father is in me, and I in the
Father.*[5]

The Word is also named Truth and Power *by
appropriation*: that is to say, in terms which can be
referred to the other Persons, but which seem
specially to belong to him, because of his procession according to knowledge. We venerate in
the Father unity, eternity and power; in the Son,
equality, beauty and wisdom. The Son is also called
Ars Dei, Life, the Ray, the Dawn, because he is the
integral manifestation of the divine Essence. It is
in him that the Father knows himself, and that we
shall one day know the Father. *He that seeth me, seeth
the Father also. If you know me, you know also my Father;
and from henceforth you know him, and you have seen
him.*[6]

The Father and the Son meet eternally in essential beatitude. They give themselves to one
another in a most intimate unity and from that
union leaps up an immaterial flame, the ardour
of infinite Love, namely the Holy Spirit. For the
act of the will produces in the one willing a new
reality, and it is this reality, subsistent and eternal in God, that is the third Person of the Blessed

[4] Isaias lxvi, 9.
[5] John x, 38.
[6] cf. John xiv, 9 and 7.

Trinity. The name Love is peculiarly his, for he is the love with which the Father loves the Son and the Son the Father. He is called *Spirit* by analogy with the life-breath which animates us, and records the rhythm of our emotions. He is the *Gift*, par excellence, for the essential character of love is to give, and the first thing that love gives is itself. Goodness is attributed to the Holy Spirit by appropriation. The Fathers also called the third Person the Divine Fire, the Spiritual Balm, the Living Source, the enjoyment and communion of the Father with the Son, for he is the embrace which consummates their union, the seal of plenitude upon the mystery of the divine processions.

St Thomas summarizes thus the cycle of the divine operations *ad intra*. 'Both in us and in God' he says, 'there is a certain cycle in the acts of the intellect and the will, for the will tends towards that which was the beginning of the understanding. But whereas in us the circle ends in that which is external—the external good moving the intellect, and the intellect moving the will, and the will by appetite and love tending to the external good— in God, the circle ends in himself. For God, by comprehending himself, conceives the Word, which is the type of all things comprehended by him (inasmuch as He comprehends all things by comprehending himself), and from this Word he proceeds to love all things and himself. Thus someone has said that "the One engenders the One, and reflects its own heat upon itself".[7]

[7] Mercurius Trismegistus: *Poemand IV.*

108

And the circle being closed, nothing more can
be added, so that a third procession is impossible'.[8]
And the Angelic Doctor concludes with a word
which opens out for us the perspective of a new
mystery, an extension and echo of the mystery of
the Blessed Trinity: 'There remains only room for
that external procession, which we call creation'.[9]

[8] St Thomas: *De Potentia Dei, Q.IX, art. 9.*
[9] ibid.

3. THE INNER LIFE OF GOD

ᗑᗐ

THESE analogies serve in a way to introduce us to the mystery of the Blessed Trinity. For now, by enlarging our noblest thoughts to infinity, we shall endeavour to arrive at some conception of the beatitude of the three uncreated Persons.

The Father expresses himself wholly in his Son, contemplating himself in the latter with infinite satisfaction. He imparts his whole substance to him, and finds himself wholly in him. And the Son in turn contemplates in the Father the inexhaustible treasure of the Essence which he is himself. *Thou art my beloved Son, in thee I am well pleased.*[1] *And all my things are thine, and thine are mine.*[2]

The Father's thought and the Son's thought are the same—unique and absolute, one truth, one expression of that truth, with the sole difference of the 'Thee' and 'Me'. *No one knoweth the Son but the Father; neither doth any one know the Father but the Son.*[3] It is, as it were, an eternal and motionless exchange of uncreated light, a perfect correspondence of knowledge and mutual recognition. *As the Father knoweth me, so I know the Father.*[4] The Son receives continuously life from the Father, and therein is all his being. *For as the Father hath life in himself, so he hath given to the Son also to have life in himself.*[5]

[1] Mark i, 11.
[2] John xvii. 10.
[3] Matthew xi, 27.
[4] cf. John x, 15.
[5] John v, 26.

When two opposing currents in an ocean meet and mix, the very violence of their embrace produces an immense wave, which seems to assault the sky. The Holy Spirit has been likened to such a wave. The Father and the Son, essentially united in the same love, form but one Source for the breathing forth of the Holy Spirit. The Spirit, who is called *Holiness of God*, proceeds from their union in the same essential unity: *Caritas de Caritate.* The life of the Father and of the Son is thus the breathing forth of the Spirit in love, and the life of the Spirit is to proceed from the Father and the Son, and therein lies the eternal superabundance of charity without end. *Charity is the bond of perfection.*[6]

This reciprocity of infinite love, in the simplicity of the same essence, is the substance of the real. All that we see or take for events or beings, what are they but an echo or faint and almost extinct reflection of that unique Reality?

So, then, the life of the three Persons can be summed up in one phrase: *God is Love.*[7] 'To be several Persons in the same divinity is nothing else than to be three with but one and the same love. It is the supreme love, but with a different property in each Person. The Person is nothing else than the supreme Love with a distinctive property'.[8] In this very nature of God, considered as subsistent Love, the same writer (and others after him) have thought to have found the most profound ana-

[6] Colossians iii, 14.
[7] 1 John iv, 16.
[8] Richard of St Victor: *De Trinitate, Bk. V, c. 20.*

111

logical reason for the divine processions. *Amor extasim facit.* 'Love does not leave the one loved in himself: it causes him to go out of himself, and enter wholly into the beloved.'[9] Without cessation, the Father goes out of himself wholly, and enters into the Son; and the Son unceasingly returns to the Father with the whole of his being, and the Father and the Son pour themselves forth in like manner into the Holy Spirit.

The Greek Fathers insisted on this mystery. They not only considered in the divine hypostases the static co-existence and the mutual compenetration, but also that eternal effusion and reflux of the Persons in the unity of the Essence. Such is the original meaning of the word *Perichoresis,* which we translate *circumincession.* It indicates 'the reciprocal circulation of one thing to another, in such a way that each attracts the other, while at the same time they are in opposition to one another'. These are, indeed, the relations of origin which constitute the Persons, and distinguish and unite them in one and the same nature. Each Person, by what is proper to himself, is then drawn wholly towards another. 'Let us admire' says one theologian, on the subject of the *Perichoresis,* 'that sublime conception which reveals to us the movement of the divine life, not only in the faculties of knowing and willing, not only in the depths of their nature, but even in the very constitution of the divine subsistents. Oh the perfect beatitude of the three Persons! Any satiety

[9] Denys the Areopogite.

is unthinkable in you, for you are not simply that placid happiness that one experiences by being in the company of another, but rather that shock of joy which comes when one has found the other, never more to part!'[10]

The Jews and the sages of pagan antiquity venerated a lone and solitary God. Revelation has taught us to adore in our God the living truth of three Persons, who co-exist in an eternal embrace. Mere human thought could never have conceived such a mystery; but having found it by a divine grace, our concept of the primal Essence has become incomparably richer and more profound. In order to accept this new and wholly divine knowledge, we must break with the categories of our natural knowledge. It was in this sense, possibly, that the prophet glimpsed the thought of God invading the earth, like the all-powerful tide of a new ocean, causing its waves to overflow its shores, overthrowing its ramparts, inundating the plains and covering the mountains. *Repleta est terra scientia Domini, sicut aquae maris operientes—for the earth is filled with the knowledge of the Lord, as the covering waters of the sea.*[11]

Note well, with Cardinal Cajetan, that in raising ourselves to God according to our natural ideas, we surely deceive ourselves if we do not pass utterly beyond them in order to lose ourselves in the abyss of the divine Essence. 'We imagine the distinction of the absolute and the relative as anterior to the divine reality, and so we think that we should place

[10] Père de Régnon.   [11] Isaias xi, 9.

it under one or other member of that division. But it is the reverse that is true. For the divine reality is anterior to the concept of being and all its distinctions. There is not in the divine reality on the one hand unity of nature and on the other, and as it were supplementarily, a trinity of Persons, but a one inexhaustible truth, one same incomprehensible secret, one same transcendent and sovereign necessity'.

FROM GOD TO MAN

1. The Unity of God's Designs

∽∽

EVERYTHING, material and spiritual, all men and each of us separately, have, from all eternity, existed in the Mind of God. The life of all of us pre-existed in the Word. *Quod factum est, in ipso vita erat.*[1] In begetting the Son, in knowing himself in the Son, God conceived us, called us and loved us from all eternity. *Pater dicendo se dicit omnem creaturam.*[2] By the Word, the Father expresses in himself all things; the Father and the Son, by the Holy Spirit, love one another and all men. Creation is thus an external reflection, an ever-changing and diffused mirror of the riches contained in the divine Essence. The universe—the divinely uttered word which vibrates and projects itself into time and space—is none other than an echo of the uncreated Word. It is his secret, the unique secret that God pronounced in what St Augustine calls 'the hymn of the six days'—*universa saeculi pulchritudo velut magnum carmen ineffabilis modulatoris*—and above all in man: for man is the resumé and conclusion of all creation.

God has only one secret, and that is his own being. What he has created for himself and himself

---

[1] John i, 3–4.   [2] St Anselm.

alone, must therefore in some way return to him. The imperfections of sin can in no way upset the divine plan, which is beyond (at the same time comprising and bringing to their final purpose) the acts of free causes in the same way as it does those of necessary causes.

Adam was created to know and love God: *Homo nexus Dei et mundi.* Man must therefore cleave to God and restore to him the world as a vast sacrifice. Still more, God raised Adam to a supernatural state, and in consequence invited him to share in his intimate life, and made all the preparations in him necessary for this return to the primal Being, which is to complete the work of creation. Adam was thus a son of God, but sin came to sever the bond of that filiation. Man's disobedience opened an abyss between God and the creature. By the promise of a Redeemer, however, God made known his mercy towards him who had offended against his justice and, from the moment of man's fall, at once began to raise him up, the Fall being but a pretext, it would seem, to reveal the splendours of the divine goodness. The demands of the sovereign justice required that a man-God, as son of man, should, as son of man, expiate man's sin and, as the Son of God, reconcile us with the Father by the infinite value of his expiation. And this wonder of love was realized. *And the Word was made flesh, and dwelt among us; and we saw his glory, the glory as it were of the only-begotten of the Father, full of grace and truth.*[3]

[3] John i, 14.

We can, in considering the realities that divine Providence has created and their order of dignity, follow, as the Apostle is constantly telling us to do, the main lines of the plan of Providence itself. It is a continuation of the divine processions in an external circle. *Amor extasim facit.* The love which causes the Father to give himself to the Son, and which the latter in the Holy Spirit returns to the Father, is the cause of both creation and redemption, with the return to the Father of those souls that are sanctified and transformed in Christ.

It is by nature that the divine processions take place. By nature the Father begets the Son, whilst both breathe forth the Holy Spirit. On the other hand, it was by a free act of the will that God decided from all eternity to create the universe, but by the same design and the same act to create it, not only by the Word but *for* the Word incarnate. The Person of Christ, indeed, is infinitely superior in dignity to all creatures, both heavenly and terrestrial, and it is in Him *de facto*, that they find their end and the very reason for their existence and consummation. The creation of man, capable of the Fall, and the glorification of the humanity of Christ—the fact that God permitted the Fall, and the will to give man a Redeemer—have never been separated in God's intention.

When we contemplate the mysteries of divine Providence and Love, let our gaze be simple. The simpler our concepts the deeper and truer they will be. For it is in the measure of their simplicity that they will approach the concepts in the Mind of God.

Whether he is creating the world or resting on the seventh day; whether he is redeeming fallen man or permitting him to share in his glory, there is no change in God. He does one thing only— *He is who is.*[4] It is his being that he contemplates and loves in his Word: *speculum sine macula.*[5] It is his Word that he looks upon with infinite complacency in Christ: *imago Dei invisibilis.*[6] It is his Christ whom he sees and loves in sanctified souls: *conformes imaginis Filii sui.*[7] It is in uttering the Word that he operates all things, and it is in this same Word that they return to his substance in the Holy Spirit. The Adam who had to leave the Garden of Eden was also a figure. His archetype—the eternal Adam and the new Man—is Christ: *Ecce Homo!*[8] *The Son of his love. . . . the image of the invisible God; the firstborn of every creature. For in him were all things created in heaven and on earth, visible and invisible, whether thrones or dominations or principalities or powers. All things were created by him and in him. And he is before all, and by him all things consist. And he is the head of the body, the church; who is the beginning, the firstborn from the dead, that in all things he may hold the primacy; because in him it hath well pleased the Father that all fulness should dwell; and through him to reconcile all things unto himself, making peace through the Blood*

---

[4] Exodus iii, 14.   [5] Wisdom vii. 26.
[6] Colossians i, 15.   [7] Romans viii, 29.
[8] John xix, 5.

of his Cross, both as to the things that are on earth and the things that are in heaven.[9]

Thus all things are restored in Christ, and gathered together again under the primacy of the Word, who rejoins eternally the Father in the breathing forth of the Spirit, in the plenitude of the Essence.

'There is need to consider in creation' says St Thomas, 'a certain cycle, according as all beings return to the Source from whom they came, so that the First Cause is also the End. All beings, therefore, must return to the End by the same causes in virtue of which they came from the Source. And just as the procession of Persons is the reason for creation, so it is also the cause of our return to the End. It is by the Son and the Holy Spirit that we have been created, and it is by them that we shall rejoin him who has made us'.[10]

[9] Colossians i, 13–20.
[10] St Thomas: *In I Sent: Dist. XIV, Q. 2.*

2. THE PERSON OF CHRIST

෴

THE second Person of the Blessed Trinity became man. He took our human nature—assumed it, in the language of the theologians—in the unity of his Person and of his being. Thus two natures subsist in Christ, but by the sole subsistence of the divine Word.

The acts which the Word accomplishes by his human nature are called *theandric*. They have the value and dignity corresponding to the Person positing them. The Son of God being infinite, the least of his acts have an infinite value, since acts are attributed to the Person—*actus sunt personarum*. The least act of the incarnate Word would thus have sufficed to redeem the whole of mankind. But the mysterious exigencies of the divine justice and love carried the Son of dilection to that excess which utterly surpasses our reckoning of reasons and causes: *supereminentem scientiae caritatem Christi*.[1] Obedient to that wisdom, mad in the eyes of men, he desired to immolate himself even to the shedding of the last drop of his most Precious Blood . . . *becoming obedient unto death, even to the death of the Cross*.[2]

[1] Ephesians iii, 19.
[2] Philippians ii, 8.

3. THE WORK OF CHRIST

ഗഗ

IN his priestly prayer after the Last Supper, Our Lord bore witness to the fact that he had made known to the world an unknown Name: *I have glorified thee on earth, I have finished the work thou gavest me to do . . . I have manifested thy Name, O Father, to men.*[1]

What is this mysterious Name? According to St Hilary and St Cyril, it is the very name of *Father.* 'The greatest work of the Son has been to make known to us the Father'.[2] The whole meaning of revelation and of redemption is comprised in this: to open to men the divine circle of the personal relations, and to draw men's souls into the stream of God's own life. Not only to make good the fault of our first parents, as one would pardon a slave a moment of revolt, but much more—to make of this unfaithful servant a child of adoption. Such is the amplitude and depth of the gesture of mercy on the part of divine Love. *In caritate perpetua dilexi te, ideo attraxi te miserans—I have loved thee with an everlasting love, therefore have I drawn thee, taking pity on thee.*[3] *Because you are sons, God hath sent the Spirit of his Son into your hearts, crying: Abba, Father. Therefore you are no longer servants but sons, and if sons, heirs also through God.*[4] *Blessed be the God and Father of our Lord Jesus Christ, who hath blessed us with spiritual blessings in heavenly places in Christ; as he*

---

[1] cf. John xvii, 4 and 6.
[2] St Hilary.
[3] Jeremias xxxi, 3.
[4] cf. Galatians iv, 6 and 7.

chose us in him before the foundation of the world, that
we should be holy and unspotted in His sight in charity.
Who hath predestinated us unto the adoption of children,
through his well-beloved Son unto himself.[5]

The incarnation of the Word is continued
through the sacraments, above all in the Holy
Eucharist. The Bread of Life is not changed into
our nature like earthly food; on the contrary, it
transforms us into him. *'Nor shalt thou convert
me, like common food, into thy substance; but thou
shalt be converted into me'.*[6] By the sacramental
life and by our life of interior prayer and contemplation, given birth to and sustained in our souls
by the sacraments, we become 'sons of the Father',
identified in some way with the Word, and truly
divinized. The Word was made flesh in order to
give to all who receive him the *power to be made the
sons of God.*[7] God became man, that men might
become God.[8]

The infinitely gentle yet powerful action of Our
Lady who loves us and protects us as her children,
develops in us this resemblance to and assimila-
tion with Christ, which makes us truly sons of the
Father. One understands better the role of Mary
as co-redemptrix if one thinks on these lines: the
whole of the supernatural life consists in our
becoming 'other Christs'. And as it belonged to
Mary and to her alone to give birth on earth to

[5] cf. Ephesians i, 3–6.
[6] St Augustine: *Confessions*, Bk. VII, 10: *Nec tu me in te
mutabis, sicut cibum carnis tuae, sed tu mutaberis in me.*
[7] John i, 12.
[8] St Augustine.

Christ, so it is by Mary, in Mary and from Mary, that we receive all spiritual gifts. It is Mary, co-redemptrix, who introduces us into the life of God. *In te et per te et de te, quidquid boni recepimus et recepturi sumus, per te recipere vere cognoscimus.*[9]

The Christian thus becomes aware that he is surrounded, enfolded and encompassed on all sides, by the divine Reality. *In ipso enim vivimus et movemur et sumus.*[10] Far more, he truly enters into this Reality, he penetrates into the very intimacy of God, he is son of the Father, not by a metaphor, not by the mere accident of a hyperbolic phrase, but as St John attests: *Behold what manner of charity the Father hath bestowed upon us, that we should be called, and should be, the sons of God—ut filii Dei nominemur et simus.*[11] *... For whom he foreknew, he also predestinated to be made conformable to the image of his Son; that he might be the firstborn among many brethren.*[12]

Jesus is thus our brother, and the Holy Spirit likewise our spirit. *Qui Spiritus Christi non habet, hic non est ejus—if any man have not the Spirit of Christ, he is none of his.*[13] It is he who speaks and prays in us, who makes known to us the mysteries of divine truth, who is our essential life, making us partake of the very breathing of God. *God hath sent the Spirit of his Son into your hearts ... For it is not you that speak, but the Spirit of your Father*

[9] ibid.
[10] Acts xvii, 28.
[11] 1 John iii, 1.
[12] Romans viii, 29.
[13] Romans viii, 9.

that speaketh in you . . . But we all, beholding the glory of the Lord with open face, are transformed into the same image from glory to glory, as by the Spirit of the Lord.[14]

By the sacred humanity of the incarnate Word the soul is raised up even to the divinity. Then will it feel crushed by the divine justice; yet drawn by his mercy it will plunge into the divine love, where it will contemplate for ever the eternal beauty, goodness and truth. Reconciled by Christ and in him, we have access to the Father in the Holy Spirit. *Per ipsum habemus accessum ambo in uno Spiritu ad Patrem—for by him we have access both in one Spirit to the Father.*[15] Here we have in a word the economy of all the divine mysteries revealed in time. Creation, incarnation, redemption, glorification—these miracles of love serve but to make known the mystery of infinite Love, one in three Persons: *the mystery which hath been hidden from ages and generations, but now is manifested to his saints.*[16]

[14] Galatians iv, 6; Matthew x, 20; 2 Corinthians iii, 18.
[15] Ephesians ii, 18.
[16] Colossians i, 26.

FROM MAN TO GOD

༄

AND so the divine life pours itself out for us with an incomprehensible liberality. If these waves of love do not penetrate our hearts it is because the latter are filled with created vanities. The divine light is completely compelling of itself, and if we are not aware of it it is because our own life, the feeble life of our *ego*, keeps us in our blindness. *Man shall not see God and live.*[1]

The first phase in our spiritual life is to empty ourselves of ourselves by a ceaseless and merciless war against every form of self-love. For sin, in sundering the bond between the Creator and the creature has destroyed the interior harmonies of the latter. Our life, separated from its Source, is utterly disorientated and disturbed. We are in revolt against God, and hence our senses are in revolt against reason.

By nature, our hearts should be turned towards God: *os homini sublime dedit.*[2] Instead, however, of keeping them in the divine light we have become earthbound, and the desire for material things has captivated us. But God made men upright, as the Scripture says: *Lo, this only have I found, that God hath made man upright.*[3] It is

[1] Exodus xxxiii, 20.
[2] Ovid: *Metamorphoses, I, 85.*
[3] cf. Ecclesiastes vii, 30.

125

in order to get back that first rectitude that we must fight against our twisted nature and our disordered senses. *I chastise my body and bring it into subjection . . . If any man will come after me, let him take up his cross daily, and follow me.*[4]

This is not the work of a day. Each one of us must climb his own Calvary step by step; must lay himself down upon the cross of sacrifice for a long agony, and endeavour with all his fallen nature to die. To this work of purification we must bring a constant, uninterrupted application, and even when we think we have at last won the day, we still have to keep a ceaseless watch over ourselves. For the lower forces of our being are ever ready to rebel, and with one moment of relaxation we shall see them regain that tyrannical domination from which we have suffered so long. With courage and determination we must drink the deathly chalice of which Christ our elder brother drank before us; and bow our heads under the sword red with the Blood of the Lamb. *Because for thy sake we are killed all the day long; we are counted as sheep for the slaughter.*[5]

But the body is not our deadliest enemy, nor the most tenacious. Sin has penetrated in us more deeply still. It is at the very centre of our mind that it has planted pride. It is there in truth that self-love hides its elusive roots; and if to all outward appearances we seem dead to self, we may

[4] 1 Corinthians ix, 27; Luke ix, 23.
[5] Psalm xliii, 22.

126

never forget that the deep germ of the evil has lost nothing of its virulence. The terrific battle between the Spirit of God and our own spirit takes place in our heart, and its issue, favourable or otherwise, will fix our destiny.

Anyone who wishes to live in keeping with his dignity as a reasonable being must undertake this struggle. The sages of antiquity have given us an example of it, but the combat in which mere nature endeavoured to triumph over itself could only end in that barely disguised self-esteem, in that vanity with which the virtue of the greatest Stoics left off. For us, the means are indicated by that Revelation which calls us to our divine inheritance, and it is from Christ alone that those means will come to us.

Perilous will be the illusion of those who think that they can, by their own efforts, raise themselves to that higher life in the supernatural order to which we are called. Most certainly we have to make every effort on our own part, but it is grace which calls forth those efforts, and accompanies and sustains them. It is grace also which crowns them. *Deus est qui operatur in nobis et velle et perficere—it is God who worketh in us, both to will and to accomplish*[6] . . . *Not by the works of justice which we have done, but according to his mercy, he saved us.*[7]

To understand this doctrine is one of the greatest favours we can receive from the liberality of the divine Master. And that knowledge of our nothingness is at the same time the freest of gifts,

6 cf. Philippians ii, 13.   7 Titus iii, 5.

and the reward which follows inevitably in proportion to our generous and sustained efforts. In the struggle with ourselves there will always be some victories, but if we push our endeavours still further, we shall understand more and more the immense task which remains for us to carry through, and the absurd inadequacy of our doubtful conquests. It is then, at last, that we turn utterly to God, certain henceforth that of ourselves we can do nothing, abandoning ourselves to his all-powerful and beneficent action. Convinced of our nothingness, we shall lose ourselves in the certitude that God is all.

Even our failures and our faults will thus become the cause and occasion of our final victory. And the tears in which we have bathed our faults will be the initial baptism of a life of abandonment and pure confidence, and our weakness will be our strength. *Gladly, therefore, will I glory in my infirmities, that the power of Christ may dwell in me . . . for when I am weak, then am I powerful . . . My grace is sufficient for thee . . . I can do all things in him who strengtheneth me.*[8]

Christ not only gives us the means to attain our end: it is through him that we must pass: *Ego sum ostium—I am the door.*[9] He himself is the Way: *I am the Way . . . no man cometh to the Father but by me.*[10]

Our intimacy with the Lamb will purify us. It is the clean of heart who will, already here below,

[8] 2 Corinthians xii, 9–10; Philippians iv, 13.
[9] John x, 9.
[10] John xiv, 6.

see God.[11] Their inner vision will begin to catch something of the eternal glory, that *light which enlighteneth every man that cometh into this world.*[12] They will at last have the strength to allow themselves to be wholly taken by God, and he who is already their Way will show himself to them as the Truth and the Life. *Now this is eternal life, that they may know thee, the only true God, and Jesus Christ whom thou hast sent.*[13]

And so, dead to ourselves, we shall begin to live in God. *Unless the grain of wheat falling into the ground die, itself remaineth alone. But if it die, it bringeth forth much fruit . . . I am the resurrection and the life; he that believeth in me, although he be dead shall live.*[14] Having overcome the trials of the first part of the way which leads to divine union, we hear the voice of the Saviour saying: *Amice, ascende superius—friend, go up higher.*[15] Then the breath of the Holy Spirit will fill our soul with gifts and virtues, which will purify it and ennoble it, like a heavenly, healing balm. *Surge, aquilo, et veni auster; perfla hortum meum et fluent aromata illius—Arise, O north wind, and come O south wind: blow through my garden, and let the aromatical spices thereof flow.*[16]

The soul is thus ready to be penetrated with

---

[11] cf. Matthew v, 8.
[12] John i, 9.
[13] John xvii, 3.
[14] John xii, 24–25; John xi, 25.
[15] Luke xiv, 10.
[16] Canticle of Canticles iv, 16.

129

the uncreated light. Illumined and ablaze with these supernatural rays, we begin already on earth to taste the inheritance of the sons of God. *That the Father of glory may give unto you the spirit of wisdom and of revelation, in the knowledge of him; the eyes of your heart enlightened, that you may know what is the hope of his calling, and what are the riches of the glory of his inheritance in the saints, and what is the exceeding greatness of his power towards us.*[17] *. . . For the Spirit himself giveth testimony to our spirit that we are the sons of God. And if sons, heirs also: heirs, indeed, of God and joint heirs with Christ; yet so, if we suffer with him, that we may be also glorified with him.*[18]

[17] Ephesians i, 17–19.
[18] Romans viii, 16–17.

MAN IN GOD

～～

WE can be, then, even in this life, as the Apostle does not cease to remind us, sons of God, and become by grace and participation what God is by nature: *divinae consortes naturae—partakers of the divine nature.*[1]

This transformation of the soul has already begun in everyone whom the sacraments have purified from sin. But in the case of those who pursue the way of sanctity to its term, it attains a mysterious consummation, which would appear to be beyond definition, for the soul no longer seems itself: *I live, now not I, but Christ liveth in me.*[2]

Arrived at this degree of union, the soul, filled with light and carried away with love, is unable to find words with which to express what it experiences. The texts of Scripture have taken on for it a new wonder and a fragrance hitherto unknown.

The divine sonship by adoption of the Christian soul is only too often a theme worn threadbare by theologians when dealing with the subject of grace. But these same propositions that endeavour to explain the prerogatives of the just sound altogether different to those who, prepared for it

[1] 2 Peter i, 4.　　　　[2] Galatians, ii, 20.

by a life of renunciation and contemplation, have personal knowledge of the divine indwelling. That divine life is like a fruit of whose bounty many get a glimpse but only those who are dead to themselves and generously faithful can taste its real sweetness. *Fructus ejus dulcis gutturi meo—his fruit was sweet to my palate.*[3] Although such a soul remains unquestionably distinct from God substantially as in operation, still it is transformed in him by faith and love. *Per fidem et caritatem sic conjungimur Christo quod transformamur in ipsum.*[4] For this reason, all that we say of the only-begotten Son absolutely, can be said by participation—that is, according to the union of love—of the sons by adoption, who have been incorporated in him.

When such souls, in the enjoyment of the divine union, speak of their interior state, it would seem sometimes—to hear them—that they think themselves freed from all the bonds which are necessarily inherent in the creature, or from that frailty which human nature can never lose while here on earth. But we have to understand the language of such souls who, forgetting themselves and being turned completely towards the divine object, are absorbed by its splendour. *If we say that we have no sin,* says St John humbly, *we deceive ourselves, and the truth is not in us.*[5] None the less, to those *who are born, not of blood, nor of the will of the flesh, nor of the will of man, but of God*

[3] Canticle of Canticles ii, 3.
[4] St Thomas on *John VI, Bk.* 7.
[5] 1 John i, 8.

is given the power *to become the sons of God.*[6] And so, inasmuch as we are born of God, and inasmuch as we have received the Holy Spirit and through him the divine life, we shall taste even now the eternal victory, which that same St John calls 'a present joy'. 'The Holy Spirit' says St Thomas, 'is a spiritual seed which proceeds from the Father, and that is why he can generate in us the divine life, and make us sons of God.'[7] *Omnis qui natus est ex Deo peccatum non facit, quoniam semen Dei manet in eo—whosoever is born of God committeth not sin, for his seed abideth in him.*[8]

In the soul that abandons itself and gives its consent to the complete sacrifice in which all love finds its fulfilment, is realized more and more fully that spiritual generation which is nothing less than a reflection altogether supernatural of the eternal generation of the Word. Such a soul no longer belongs to earthy generations: it is no longer a child of the flesh, nor of its own will, but moment by moment is born of God. It lives the divine life; it knows God with the knowledge whereby God knows himself, and loves him with the love with which he loves himself. It is changed into Truth, into perfect praise; it is uttered with the Word. And, finally, it conforms to the archetype included from all eternity in the divine Mind. It is exactly what God wills. In it is verified the prophetic word of the inspired Book: *I shall dwell in thee because I have chosen thee; thou shalt be my rest for all eternity. As*

[6] John i, 12–13.
[7] St Thomas on *Epist. to the Romans VIII.*
[8] 1 John iii, 9.

the bridegroom rejoices over the bride, so shall thy God rejoice over thee.[9]

A soul transformed in Christ is obedient. Its submission to the Father is spontaneous like the beating of its heart. It follows the divine inspiration without deviation or calculation, with a movement so direct and so prompt that the world marvels at it. For the ways of the world are complicated, and the steps of human prudence are uncertain. But he who dwells in perfect humility is completely pliant under the mysterious breath of the Spirit. *For whosoever are led by the Spirit of God, they are the sons of God.*[10]

The soul hears the voice of the Master: *Maria audiebat verbum Domini.*[11] It gives itself up to that occupation, of which it will never more be deprived:... *qui non auferetur ab ea.*[12] Far removed from earthy cares, it is wholly abandoned to the divine will and altogether silent. So silent that it may forget itself, forget the name by which it is known. *Thou shalt be called by a new name, which the mouth of the Lord shall name... thou shalt be called My Pleasure in thee, because the Lord hath been well pleased with thee.*[13]

This multiplication of life is a kind of perpetual miracle, of which all other miracles are only a figure. Divine love is reproduced in souls and, without in any way being divided in itself or exhausted, pours out upon them its essential

[9] cf. Isaias lxii, 5.
[10] Romans viii, 14.
[11] Luke x, 39.
[12] Luke x, 42.
[13] cf. Isaias lxii, 2 and 4.

134

treasure. Every child of God receives the fulness of the graces of which it stands in need, and can expect its desire to be balanced by the light it receives.

True, the act of a creature remains finite, but the divine object which it enjoys in that fulness is infinite. That is why the soul is, as it were, saturated and, according to the word of the contemplatives, 'seems to have all the rights and all the prerogatives of the only Son of God'.[14] 'It now only sees unity.'[15] *My dove, my perfect one, is but one.*[16] All the divine secrets of which such a soul is guardian, all the graces with which it is enriched, are for it comprised in this single phrase: *This is my beloved Son.*[17]

We live, it is true, in a world of enigmas. God dwells in us in a manner always hidden. It is in a deep shadow that, by his love, he manifests himself to souls who live in union with him. Theologians speak very truly of a 'hidden experience which, although obscure, makes us feel that our soul is living in contact with a higher life, permitting us to enjoy really and truly the presence of the divine Persons';[18] but 'through a veil which will never be torn here below'. It is given to us to 'taste God'—*pati divina*—experimentally;[19] but only in a dark manner. The beloved is present

---

[14] Consummata.
[15] Suso.
[16] Canticle of Canticles vi, 8.
[17] Matthew iii, 17.
[18] John of St Thomas *in I.P. q.43. Disp. 17, no. 14.*
[19] Ibid, no. 12.

to us, as the Canticle of Canticles says, *quasi stans post parietem—behind the wall.*[20] *Truly, thou art a hidden God.*[21]

Nevertheless, the soul, docile to the teachings of divine Love, understands the word of Christ: *All things whatsoever I have heard of my Father, I have made known to you.*[22] In faith, in the impenetrable depths of pure faith, God gives to the soul a present-ment of those truths hidden in himself, which will one day be our beatitude. This 'all' that Jesus makes known to us, says St Gregory the Great, 'are the interior joys of charity and the delights of heaven that he discloses to us day by day by the inspirations of his love. By the fact that we love all the joys of heaven, we already know them; for love itself is knowledge: *quia ipse amor notitia est.*

I will give thee hidden treasures and the concealed riches of secret places . . . The wisdom of God in a mystery, a wisdom which is hidden, which God ordained before the world, unto our glory . . . that eye hath not seen, nor ear heard, nor has it entered into the heart of man . . . to us God hath revealed them by his Spirit. For the Spirit searcheth all things, yea the deep things of God.[23]

This wisdom is the reflection in the intellect of the love with which the soul is altogether pene-trated, like a fire which consumes and divinizes. *In fuoco amor me mise.* Or, better, as St Catherine

[20] Canticle of Canticles ii, 9.
[21] Isaias xlv, 15.
[22] John xv, 15.
[23] Isaias xlv, 3; 1 Corinthians ii, 7–10.

of Siena says: *La mia natura è fuoco.* It is enough to be on fire in order to cause other fires, near and far. *For many waters cannot quench charity . . . the lamps thereof are fire and flames.*[24] *I am come to cast fire on the earth, and what will I but that it be kindled.*[25] *Our God is a consuming fire.*[26]

That such souls should produce nothing in the eyes of men, or that they should spend themselves in a thousand works, means nothing to them. Indeed, they do but one thing: they live in God. Such is their work. It is the Father who works in them: *Pater in me manens, ipse facit opera—the Father who abideth in me, he doth the works.*[27]

Such souls, then, are 'simple with the Simple'; and if they gaze deep within themselves discover there an abyss of simplicity that nothing can disturb. It is just that simplicity which constitutes their treasure and strength, and their inexhaustible joy. They rest in the purity of God. *Who will give me wings like a dove, and I will fly and be at rest.*[28] *Be ye simple as doves.*[29]

And it is because it is simple that the soul is still. No one in this life is absolutely proof against temptations and faults, but when, by an excess of divine goodness, our gaze penetrates the mystery of the divine filiation in us, we cannot feel fear. *Fear is not in charity.*[30] *I am sure that neither death nor life . . . shall be able to separate us*

[24] Canticle of Canticles viii, 6–7. [25] Luke xii, 49.
[26] Deuteronomy iv, 24. [27] John xiv, 10.
[28] Psalm liv, 7. [29] Matthew x, 16.
[30] 1 John iv, 18.

137

from the love of God, which is in Christ Jesus, Our Lord.[31]

A soul given over to divine Love possesses this intoxicating knowledge: that its enemies are only mortal; that is to say, things which are not. And he whom it has taken for a friend and lover, who is its centre and form, its all and only love, is *he who is.*[32] Such a soul laughs, with the Apostle, at life and death, at the present and future, at principalities and powers, for its joy is vaster than all the oceans, and its peace deeper than all the depths.

The spirit of man longs to pass beyond finite things. It can only breathe freely if it can at last raise itself above time and number and space. We are frail, and our eyes are weak until they are turned towards the Sun of Being. But when the intellect is at last replete with eternity, it finds again that 'delightful health', that equilibrium of our first parents, for which it has felt so persistently a mysterious longing. *Being rooted and founded in charity, we are able to comprehend with all the saints what is the breadth and length and height and depth: to know also the charity of Christ, which surpasseth all knowledge . . . we are filled unto all the fulness of God.*[33] The influence radiating from these centres of charity is incalculable, for by virtue of their union with Christ, such souls are the spouses of the King: they save the world.

[31] Romans viii, 38–39.
[32] Exodus iii, 14.
[33] Ephesians iii, 17–19.

And thus, by acting solely in God and with and for him, the man of prayer places himself at the centre of hearts. His influence is world-wide: he gives to all the fulness of grace with which he himself is filled. *He that believeth in me, as the Scripture saith: out of his belly shall flow rivers of living water.*[34] *Now this he said,* adds St John, *of the Spirit, which they should receive who believed in him.*[35] Having become perfect man, he sees accomplished in himself the desire of humanity; one with Christ, he becomes, so to speak, the well-Beloved himself, *the desire of the everlasting hills.*[36]

With much more reason than the Latin poet can he say that he is a man, and that nothing human is foreign to him.[37] He possesses treasures for all who are in need; wine and milk for all who thirst; sacred and healing balm for all who are wounded.

He who is lost in the embrace of the divine Essence, who allows himself to be born anew together with Christ according to the will of the Father, becomes, indeed, a consoler of souls. He gives to others, expecting no return, the eternal happiness with which he is aflame. He enlightens and warms the world, because his only care is for God. He can apply to himself the prophetic words: *The Spirit of the Lord is upon me, because*

[34] John vii, 38.
[35] John vii, 39.
[36] Genesis xlix, 26.
[37] *Homo sum: humani nihil a me alienum puto.* Terence: *Heauton* I, 1.25.

*the Lord hath anointed me. He hath sent me to preach
to the meek, to heal the contrite of heart, and to preach
release to captives and deliverance to them that are in
bondage.*[38]

He who possesses God possesses in him everything—the archangels, the grains of dust, the
centuries past and to come. So St Thomas does not
hesitate to apply to the sanctified soul the words
of the Psalmist: *Thou hast subjected all things
under his feet,*[39] as we read in the passage in his
Commentary on the Epistle to the Corinthians
where he explains the verse: *For all things are
yours . . . whether it be . . . the world, or life, or death, or
things present or things to come.*[40]

The stability of a soul that has truly found God
in itself and is buried in him, defies all created
powers. Henceforth, it is placed in the single
centre where the lines of the strength of divine
Providence converge. Formerly, it depended upon
circumstances and events, but it would seem that
now all things serve and obey it. 'All that comes
to pass' says the Angelic Doctor,[41] 'serves the
universal order, and that is why nothing exists
which has not as its end these heights, the won-
ders of which surpass all creation . . .' It is to the
saints of God that we can apply those words in
the Gospel: *Super omnia bona sua constituet eum,*[42]
and St Paul's: *We know that to them that love*

[38] cf. Isaiah lxi, 1.
[39] Psalm viii, 8.
[40] 1 Corinthians iii, 22.
[41] St Thomas: *In Ep. ad Rom. VIII.*
[42] Matthew xxiv, 47.

God all things work together unto good; to such as, according to his purpose, are called to be saints.[43]

The mind, entirely penetrated by the light of the Word, henceforth enjoys a great liberty. It is raised above the judgments and opinions of the world for, in the light in which God has established it, the foolishness of these things appears to it with a clearness which allows of no hesitation. *The Lord knoweth the thoughts of men that they are vain . . . And you shall know the truth, and the truth shall make you free.*[44] Thus transformed, the soul dominates the fluctuations of selfishness and interested complacences. It has no more regrets, no consolations that it can call its own. Its only aim and desire now is the greater glory of God, and it seeks with all its strength to serve him. *For what have I in heaven, and besides thee what do I desire upon earth.*[45]

The soul thus divinized lives in a sacred depth, for its life is buried with Christ in God: *Vita vestra abscondita est cum Christo in Deo.*[46] Such a one is hidden from the sight of men but knows himself known to God, just as he knows that God recognizes himself in him: *Sicut novit me Pater, et ego agnosco eum—as the Father knoweth me, and I know the Father.*[47] The Holy Spirit now makes him say unceasingly *Abba, Father,* and his

[43] Romans viii, 28.
[44] Psalm xciii, 11; John viii, 32.
[45] Psalm lxxii, 25.
[46] Colossians iii, 3.
[47] John x, 15.

141

whole life is given to recognizing this Paternity. That word from the depths of his soul is the offering the Father accepts above all others. *As the Father hath taught me these things, I speak, and he hath not left me alone. For I do always the things that please him.*[48]

All souls ennobled with the dignity of sons of God are one in the communion of saints, and thereby form the Mystical Body of Christ. Each of them represents the whole human race; each one is a Christ. And their union, even in this life, constitutes but one Christ, the only-begotten Son, in whom all things are gathered and return to the Father. *Particeps sum omnium timentium te—I am a partaker with all them that fear thee*[49] ... *That he might make known unto us the mystery of his will, according to his good pleasure which he hath purposed in him; in the dispensation of the fulness of times, to re-establish all things in Christ, that are in heaven and on earth, in him. In whom we also are called ... to be unto the praise of his glory.*[50]

This is the dawn of eternal life. That life, which the transformed soul begins even in this life, is a participation in the life of the most Blessed Trinity. Of the inner secrets of that mysterious communication of the divine life we have, when all is said and done, explained nothing. Nor will we attempt to do so of ourselves, or stretch out an over-bold hand towards the veil which hides the glory of the sanctified soul.

[48] John viii, 28 and 29.   [49] Psalm cxviii, 63.
[50] Ephesians i, 9–12.

Super omnem gloriam protectio—for over all the glory shall be a protection.[51] To attempt to write in unsanctioned words the absolute character of that eternal union which silent love demands, anticipates and possesses even now, would be a profanation. Let us, then, allow him whom the Church calls the Mystical Doctor to utter the words which will leave us at the threshold of the ultimate secret.

'It is only in heaven that the soul will know God as it is known by him, and love him as it is loved by him. Then, indeed, will its love be none other than the love of God itself . . . Then will the soul love with the will and strength of his love . . . and there will be only one love, namely the love of God. Until the soul arrives at this consummation, it is not satisfied. . . .'

'It is by the Holy Spirit' continues the same Mystical Doctor, 'that the soul in heaven will be able to breathe in God with the same aspiration of love which the Father breathes with the Son and the Son with the Father, which is the Holy Spirit himself . . . For the soul's consummation would not be a true and total one, were it not transformed in the three Persons of the Blessed Trinity, in a clear and manifest manner. And even when that communication is received in this life, no mortal tongue can describe it, for the soul, united with God and transformed in him, breathes God in God, and that aspiration is that of God himself.'[52]

---

[51] Isaias iv, 5.
[52] St John of the Cross: *Spiritual Canticle*, stanza 38.

'As soon as God has bestowed upon the soul so great a favour as to unite it to the most Blessed Trinity, whereby it becomes like unto God and God by participation, is it altogether incredible that it should exercise the faculties of its understanding and perform its acts of knowledge and love—or, to speak more accurately, should have it all done in the Trinity together with It—as the Blessed Trinity Itself? Is it not in order to allow the soul to attain to such a life that God created it in his own image and likeness? But no knowledge, no intellectual power can explain that mystery... Yet the Son of God has obtained for us such a grace, in giving us the power to become children of God. It was his express request of the Father: *Father, I will that where I am, they also whom thou hast given me may be with me.*[53] Which is the same as saying that they (the souls) may do by participation in the Blessed Trinity what Jesus does naturally: that is, breathe the Holy Spirit'.[54]

And Jesus goes on to say: *Not for them only do I pray, but for them also who through their word shall believe in me: that they all may be one, as thou, Father, in me and I in thee, that they also may be one in us... I in them, and thou in me, that they may be made perfect in one. I pray for them whom thou hast given me, for they are thine. All that is mine is thine, and thine is mine, and I am glorified in them... Holy Father, keep*

[53] John xvii, 24.
[54] St John of the Cross: *Spiritual Canticle*, stanza 39.

*them in thy Name, whom thou hast given me, that they
may be one as we also are one.*[55]

*The Spirit and the Bride say: Come. And he that
heareth, let him say: Come . . . Behold I come quickly,
and my reward with me. Amen: come, Lord Jesus . . .*[56]

[55] cf. John xvii, 9–11; 20–23.
[56] cf. Apocalypse xxii, 17–20.

Printed in the United Kingdom
by Lightning Source UK Ltd.
123750UK00001B/216/A

9 780852 446737